WALLACE BERMAN
OFF THE GRID

TOTAH

DAVID TOTAH

in conversation with

TOSH BERMAN

DT **When you think of your father, Wallace Berman, what are the first things that come to mind?**

TB A day doesn't go by where I don't have some thoughts on Wallace, or my mom, Shirley. Death is, in many ways, the period at the end of the sentence. Still, there is always something new to discover or expand on. And I think that the first thing that comes to my mind is how deep or complex Wallace was within his world, but also at or on my side of life. There is the odd duality of thinking of Wallace and his artwork, as well as private memories of him—like nervously shaking his leg when he was reading and sitting in a chair.

DT **Are there any works of his that you revisit again and again in your mind, works that stay with you longer than others?**

TB Wallace made a piece of work called *You've Lost That Lovin' Feelin'*, which is the Righteous Brothers song that was produced and cowritten by Phil Spector. Phil came by Wallace's studio and bought that work. I often think of where the work is now that Phil is dead. I have to believe that the Spector Estate is in a mess of some sort. Still, I haven't seen the work since the 1990s in Amsterdam, when Wallace had a retrospective at the ICA there. Another piece that comes to mind is the box he made for Brian Jones of the Rolling Stones. I'm not sure if Brian has even seen the work. I believe that Keith Richards had it, but it was purchased by Charles Cowles, who was the publisher of *Artforum* and had a gallery in New York. He had trouble obtaining that work from Keith, if I'm not mistaken.

DT **What role does chance play in his work?**

TB I think chance had a minimal role in his overall work. I think he believed in the creative process that "chance" could bring, but being with him in his studio almost daily, I would see him working out his art in a very thorough manner. It took him a long time to compose a piece, and he wasn't a fast worker, but he did work seven days a week.

DT **There is a darkness and a light in so much of his work; did you have a sense of those polarities when you were growing up around him?**

TB Wallace was both dark and light at the same time. He had a wicked sense of humor, and he appreciated humor in all its twisted forms, but there was also a sense of darkness in both his work and life. The yin and yang aspects are equal partners, and Wallace always had the shade of darkness, but a sense of joy came with it. He recognized the absurdity of life, especially for one who was born and raised in the twentieth century.

DT **How do you see Wallace as a person in the work that he made?**

TB I don't separate Wallace from his work/art. He pretty much put all of himself into the art, and I think his being such a private person was his signature, or his touch. If you have a Wallace work in your life or in the house, you also have a percentage of his soul.

DT **What impact has his legacy had on you?**

TB "Legacy" is such a deathlike word. My impression of him keeps moving, like the tide, or a wave hitting the beach over and over again. It's the same journey, but there are nuances and slight changes, which make you reflect on more than one thought or thing in his life. If anything, I picked up from him that you should always work on your art or craft and never stop progressing or moving. Don't be afraid of changes, but keep your eyes open in case something appears in front of you.

DT **Do you feel that when he was making work, he had a particular audience in mind?**

TB No. I don't think Wallace thought that much of the viewer or audience. He liked the exchange between the viewer and the artwork. But again, he didn't have the physical or spiritual need to show his work. I think his doing art was very much a conversation between him and his work. So, in such a fashion, I think he had the same communication as one who sees his work as well. I think they may share the same landscape or platform.

DT **What relationship does the film *Aleph* have to other work, like *Semina* and the Verifax series?**

TB For me, I can't separate Wallace's work into separate or different mediums. It's all Wallace. Each medium serves its purposes or has its limits. The film *Aleph* is work on an 8mm film. Blowing it up to 16mm film changes the format a touch. The Verifax works are in a different medium and have their limitations and space. *Semina*, the publication that he put out, is very much a precious object, as well as something valuable and practical. It was his show-and-tell, where he could share his taste in poets and visuals with others. In his mind, *Semina* wasn't meant for everyone, but only for those to whom he gave copies. It was an intimate relationship between him as the artist/editor and the reader/viewer.

DT **What do you think Wallace would make of his work gathered together in an exhibition, all these years later?**

TB In all honesty, I don't think there is an answer to that. I can only know what Wallace Berman, 1976, would or would not do. I think he would avoid gallery solo shows and maybe do only museum exhibitions. But then again, it depends on his relationship with that future gallerist or gallery. If it's a gallery situation, he would put the show together himself and do the design work for the announcements. He was very much a control freak regarding his art and how it was displayed on a wall or in a space. In my mind, as his son, and controlling his estate, there is the live Wallace and the Wallace after he passed away. I have to deal with the issues of today and be aware of the history, but things do change.

DT **Considering *Semina* and the community of artists Wallace collected around him, what do you think his message to young artists would be in today's context?**

TB One of his significant contributions to the future art landscape is the importance of doing things yourself—DIY. I think he would have approved of the punk era, because it was an era of making one's own zines and broadsheets, of all sorts. He liked the poetry community for the same reasons, because of their broadsheets, journals, and indie-like publishing. Wallace basically said I could make a publication and give it out free, with no concern over budget or money issues. A very one-to-one approach to making such a publication. He went by his own rules in making art, and I think other artists greatly admire that sense of freedom, of not playing by someone else's game or master plan.

DT **Do you know if he had a mentor at some point, someone who inspired him at the beginning, when he started making art?**

TB Wallace never talked about this, but I believe he didn't have a physical mentor around him, or someone he asked for advice. He was a great admirer of artists like Marcel Duchamp and Jean Cocteau—which is an interesting duality. Cocteau and Duchamp seem to be exact opposites, yet Wallace was drawn to both artists. He met Duchamp at the Pasadena retrospective put together by Walter Hopps in 1963, and my dad was a fan of his work way before that meeting. And he never met Cocteau. He did correspond with Herman Hesse, who wrote *The Glass Bead Game* and *Steppenwolf*. So maybe that was a mentorship of some sort?

DT **Who were the authors and what were the books that had an impact on him and his work?**

TB *Steppenwolf* by Herman Hesse was an essential book for Wallace. He purchased numerous remaindered copies of that book at Pickwick Book Shop on Hollywood Boulevard during the 1950s. He gave copies out as gifts to people. He loved literature produced by the surrealists and the Dada movement. And he had a thing for Baudelaire, Rimbaud, and Mallarmé. Poetry fueled his imagination, and he was friends with poets, but he also read a great deal of poetry and kept up with that world through various small-press publications and journals.

DT **He was very open and oriented toward European literature, poetry, et cetera... Hesse, Cocteau, et cetera. How do you see that influence/inspiration in his work?**

TB Wallace, on one level, was very American in character, but his taste in films and literature was European. He read *View* magazine as a teenager and young adult, a surrealist publication that came out in New York City during the 1940s. Many of the artists and poets of that time lived in Manhattan due to the war overseas. The surrealist imagination, or approach to the creative spirit, profoundly affected Wallace and his art. He never took anything at face value or accepted it as it was/is but, more likely, put himself into that type of structure or work. And that I think is a very strong American character, where one feels, "I can do that."

DT **What was his routine, day to day, for his work?**

TB Wallace worked seven days a week, with no days off. He would go into his work space or studio daily, and almost kept regular work hours while doing or making art. He would come back to the house to either have lunch, take a nap, or read a book or publication. But then it was back to work, until the early evening. And some evenings, he would spend time in his creative space. He was a very disciplined man to a certain degree.

DT **What did repetition mean to Wallace?**

TB Meditation, and just floating with the drone sound of a music piece, or seeing images telling a narrative, in multiple ways. He could pick up a riff and take it as far as he wanted to.

DT **What was Shirley's influence on his work and his life? Was he showing her his new work as soon as it was finished?**

TB Shirley would look or go over Wallace's work. He would share the work once it was finished, to get feedback or her impressions of the work. My mom told me a story before she passed away in which Wallace came from the studio and was visually upset, because he felt he had nothing more to say, or his inspiration had left him. As he moaned and groaned, Shirley just told him to shut up and go back to the studio and work. He did so, and did no more complaining about the process.

DT **Was she always supportive of him and his work? Was he asking her what she thought of a new work he had just made?**

TB It took me a while, but I realized Shirley was also an artist. She wanted to go to art school in San Francisco, and she got financing from the school system to do so, but her father refused her request, because she was a girl, and a girl needed just a high school education. She was crushed, and to her dying day I could tell she was deeply disappointed in what had happened to her. Beyond that, she chose to live an artist's life with my father. So she was one hundred percent supportive of his work and life.

"Most intellectuals and most artists belong to the same type. Only the strongest of them force their way through the atmosphere of the bourgeois earth and attain the cosmic."

—Hermann Hesse, *Steppenwolf*

Untitled, c. 1968
Verifax collage
37.25 × 33 inches (94.5 × 83.5 cm)

"Most intellectuals and most artists belong to the same type. Only the strongest of them force their way through the atmosphere of the bourgeois earth and attain the cosmic."

—Hermann Hesse, *Steppenwolf*

Untitled, c. 1968
Verifax collage
37.25 × 33 inches (94.5 × 83.5 cm)

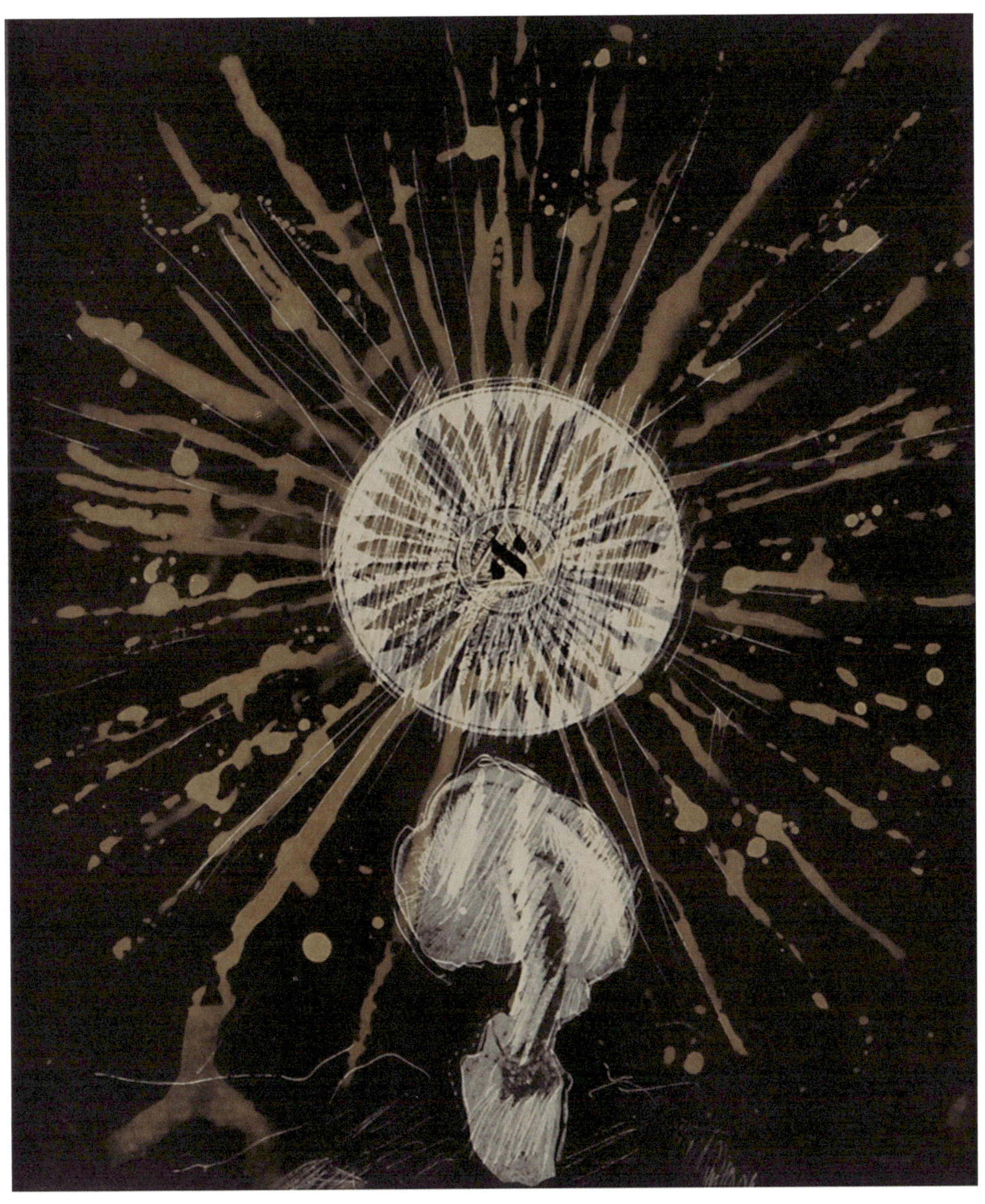

Untitled (Ray Charles, This Is the Card That Reads 7), c. 1965
collage
12.5 × 8.5 inches (31.75 × 21.5 cm)

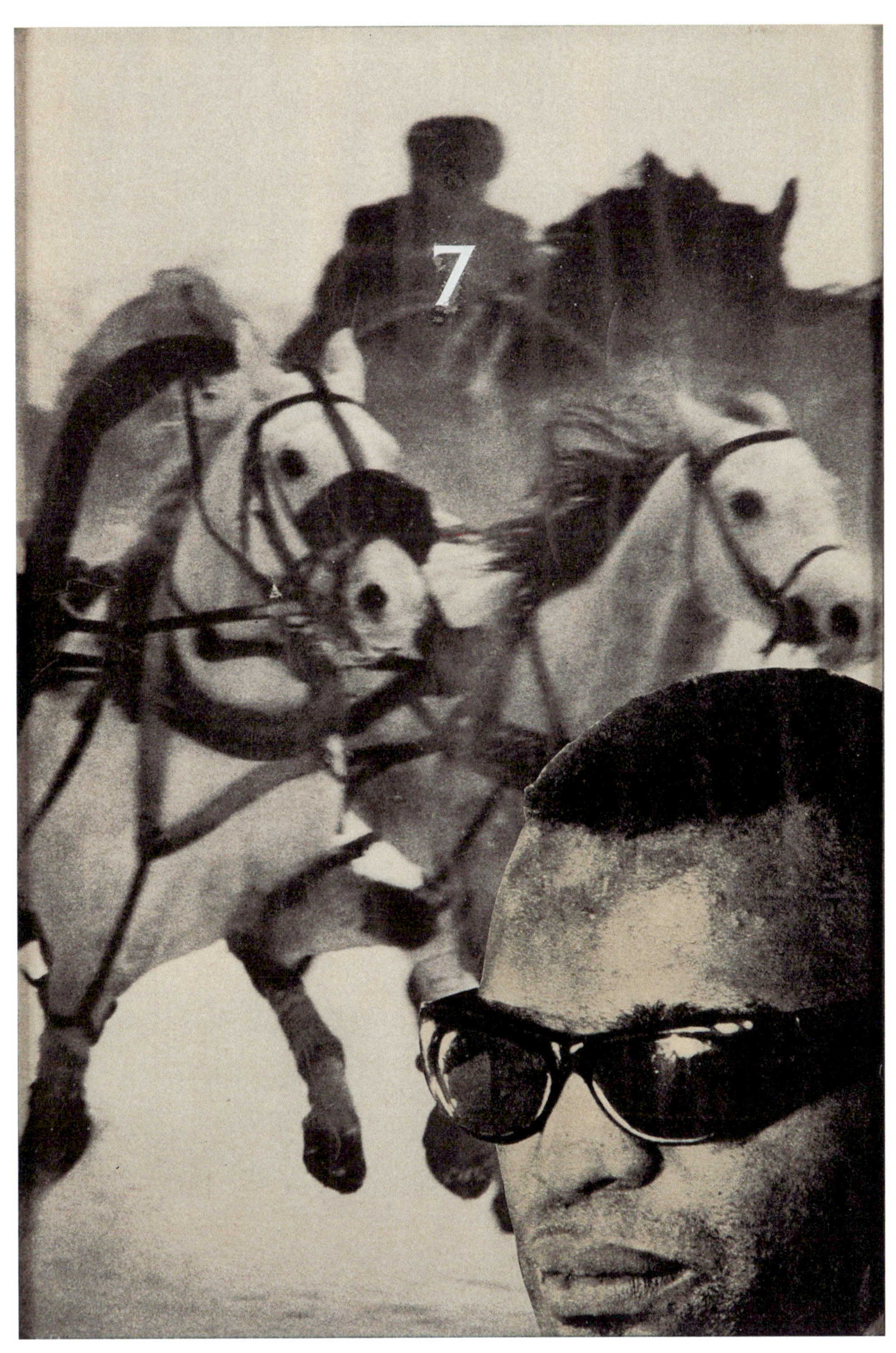
7

Untitled (Proof, Yalta and Broads in Beige), c. 1965
Verifax collage with proof stamp
5 × 7.5 inches (12.70 × 19 cm)

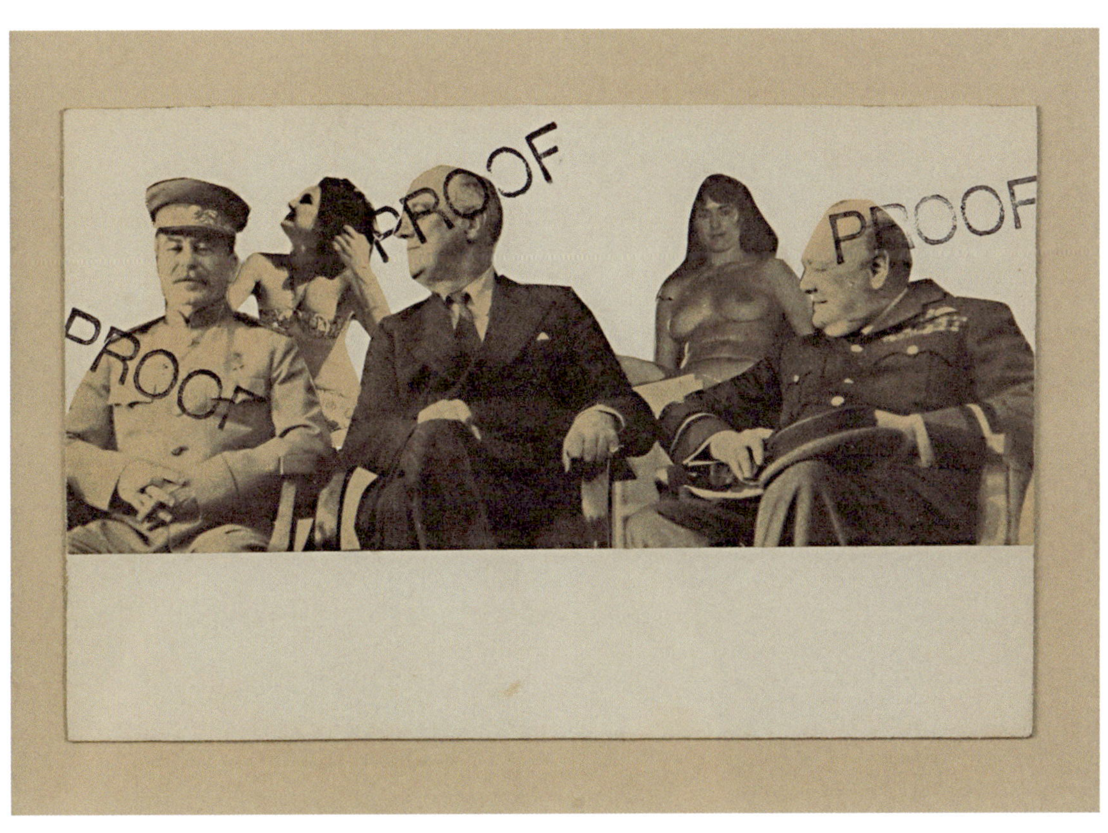
PROOF
PROOF
PROOF

Untitled, 1964–76
acrylic, Verifax collage, and transfer lettering on board
13 × 10.25 inches (33 × 26 cm)

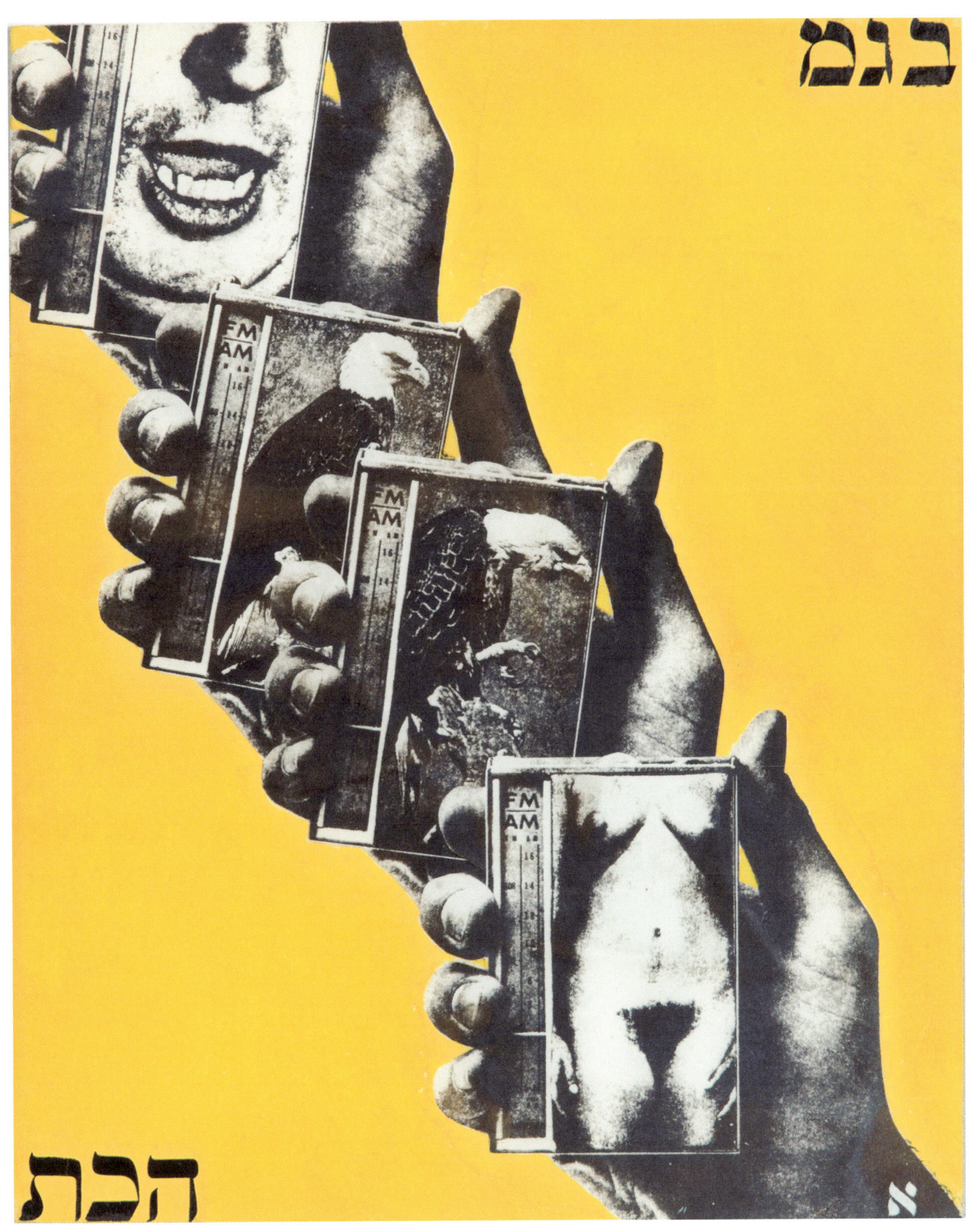
בגמ
FM
AM
הבת
א

Untitled (Business Man at Desk), c. 1965
Verifax collage
7 × 7 inches (17.75 × 17.75 cm)

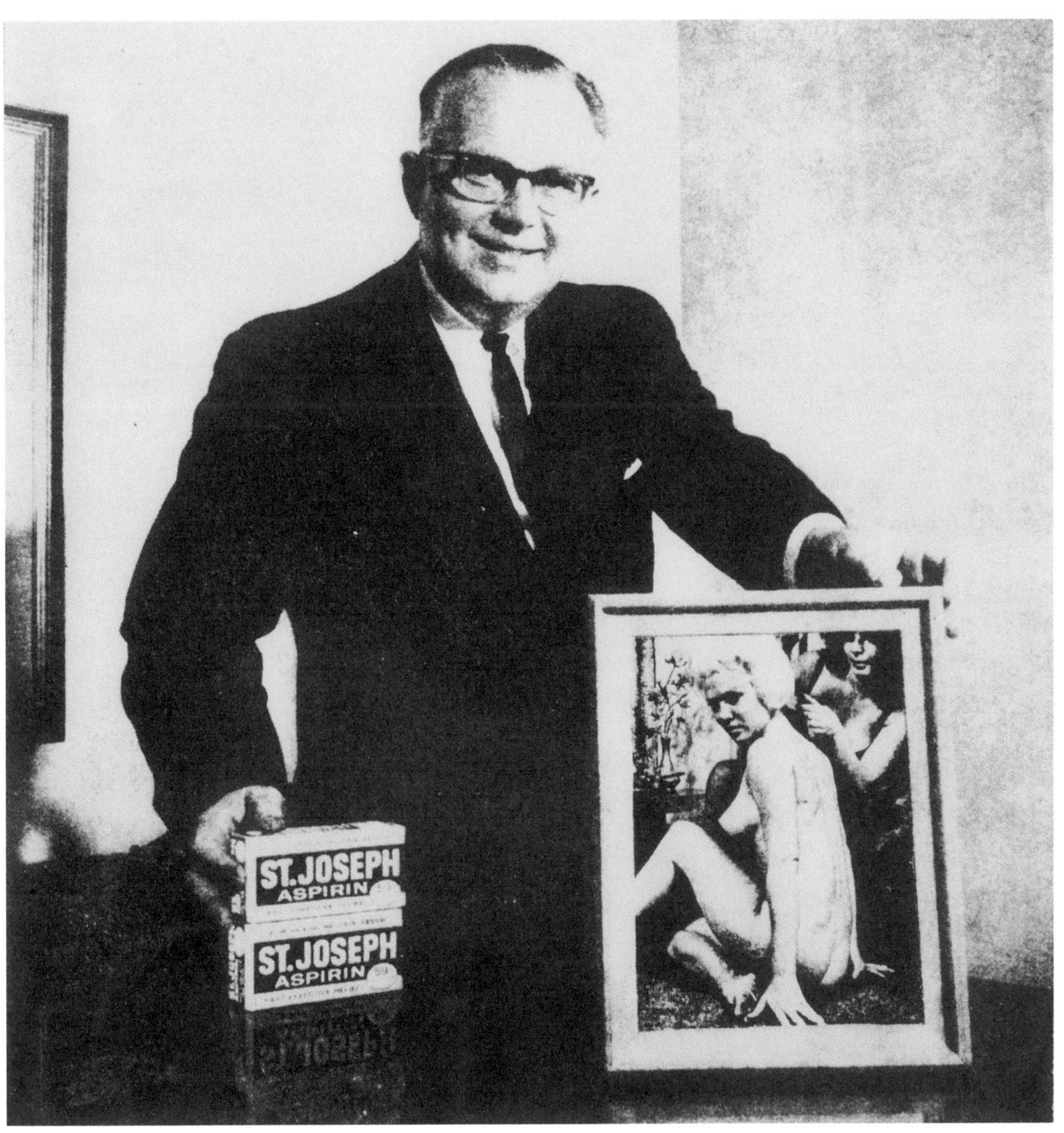
ST. JOSEPH
ASPIRIN
ST. JOSEPH
ASPIRIN

Untitled (Moonscape with 3 Arrows), 1964–76
Verifax collage with writing
18.25 × 9 inches (46.5 × 21 cm)

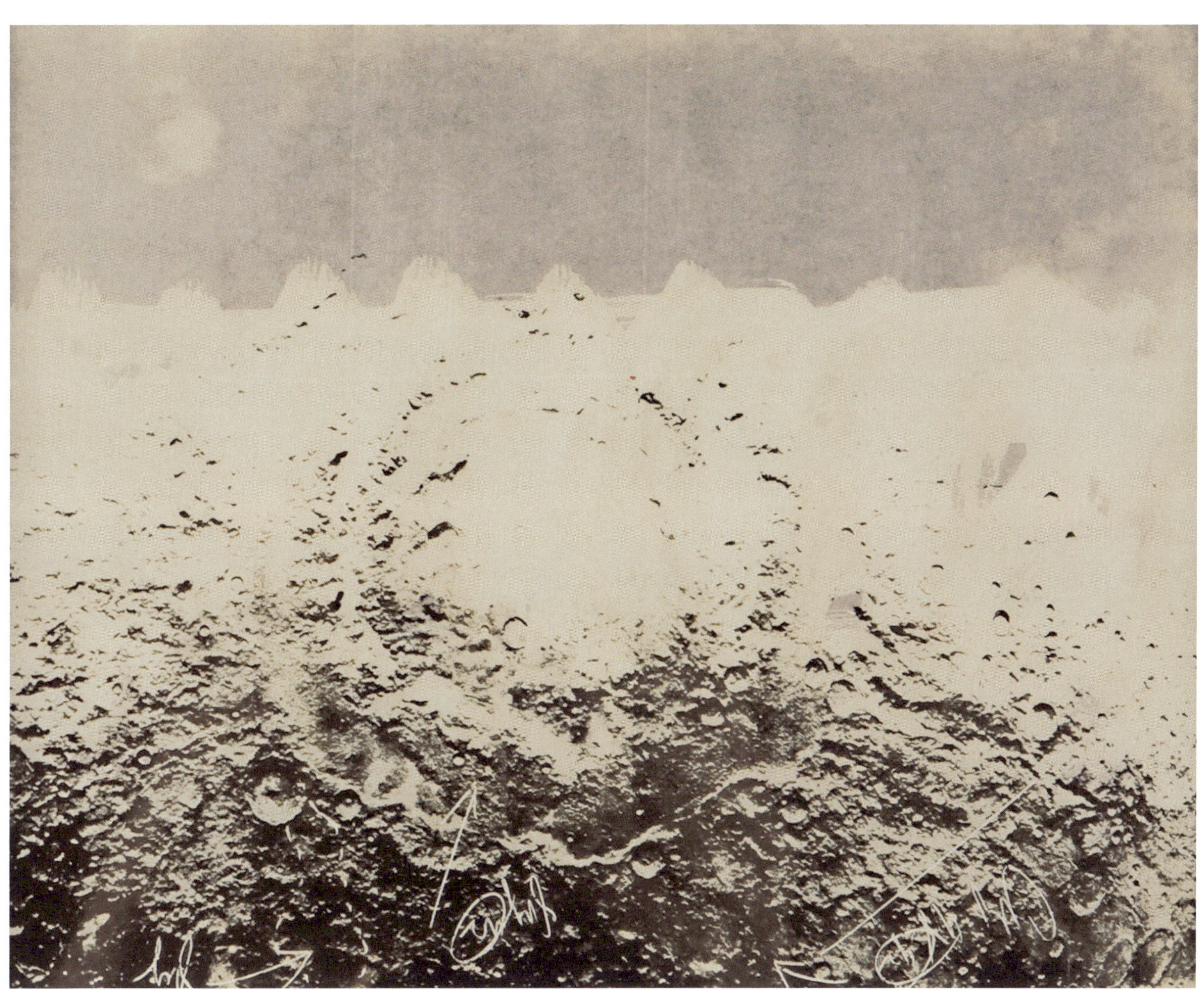

Untitled (Louis Armstrong/Syringe in mouth), 1946
print
13 × 11.25 inches (33 × 28.5 cm)

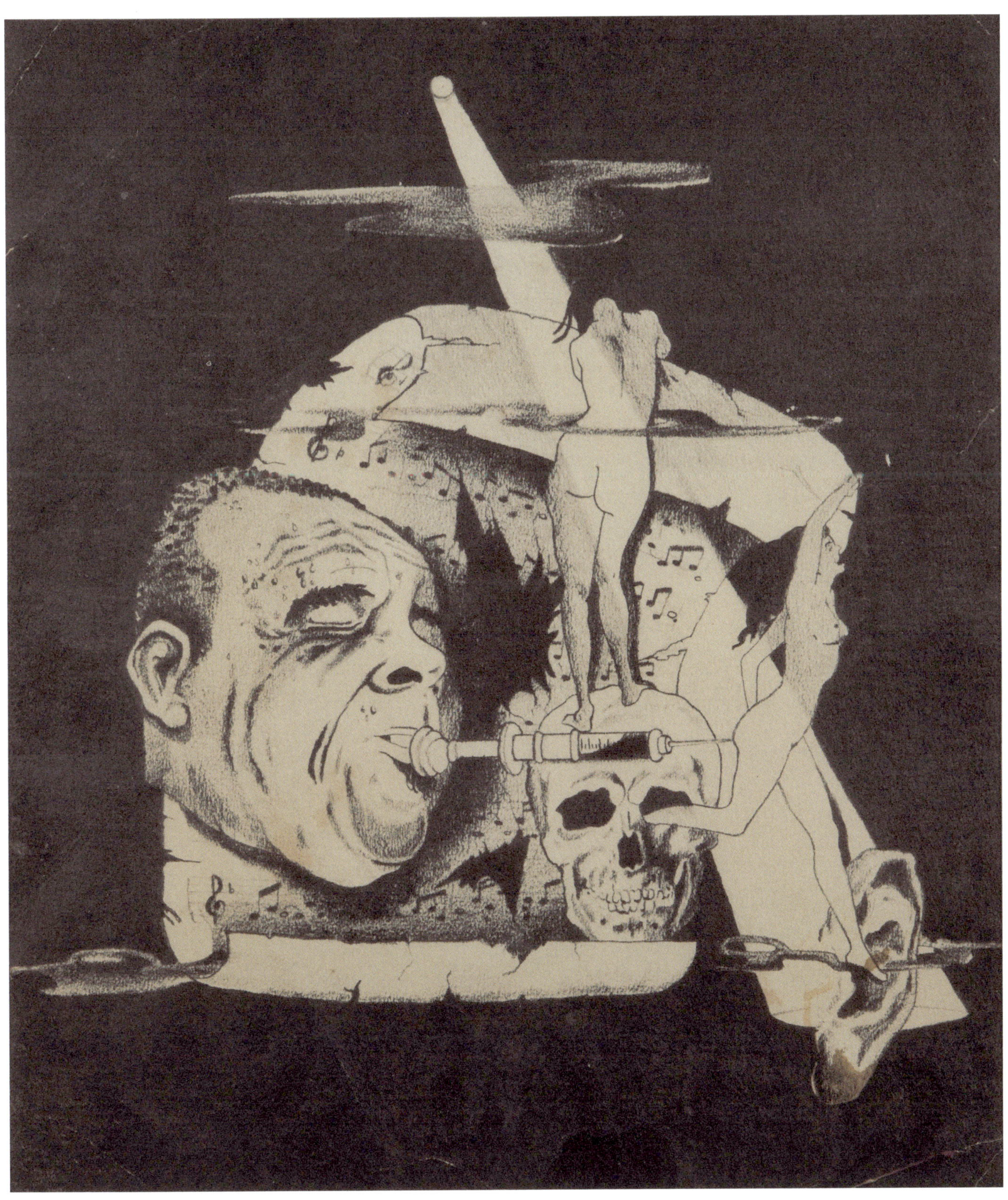

Untitled, 1964–76
Four-part negative Verifax collage
13 × 14 inches (33.02 × 35.56 cm)

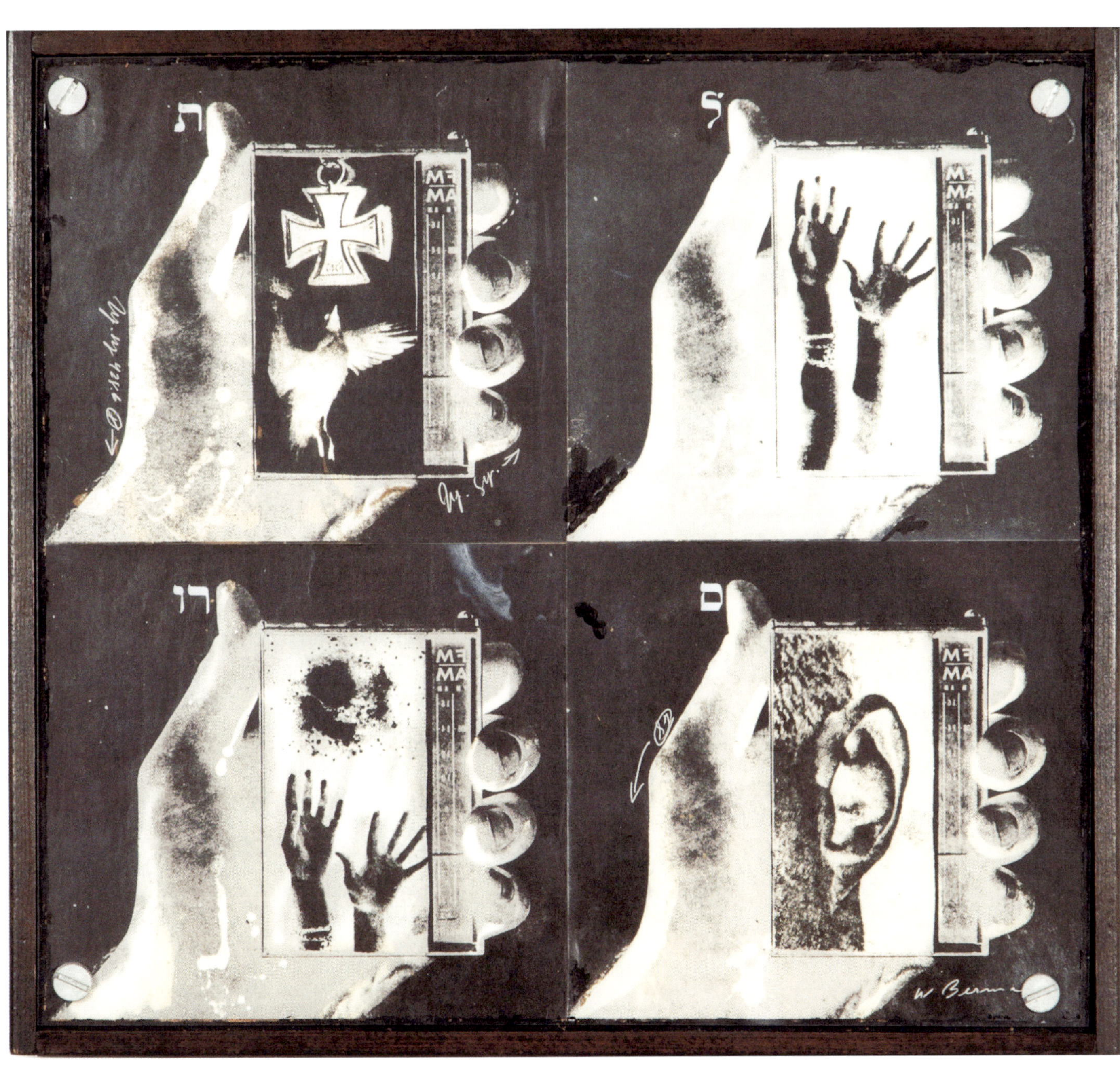

Untitled (C3-Cross), c. 1975
Twenty-five-part negative Verifax collage
33.5 × 30.5 inches (85 × 77.5 cm)

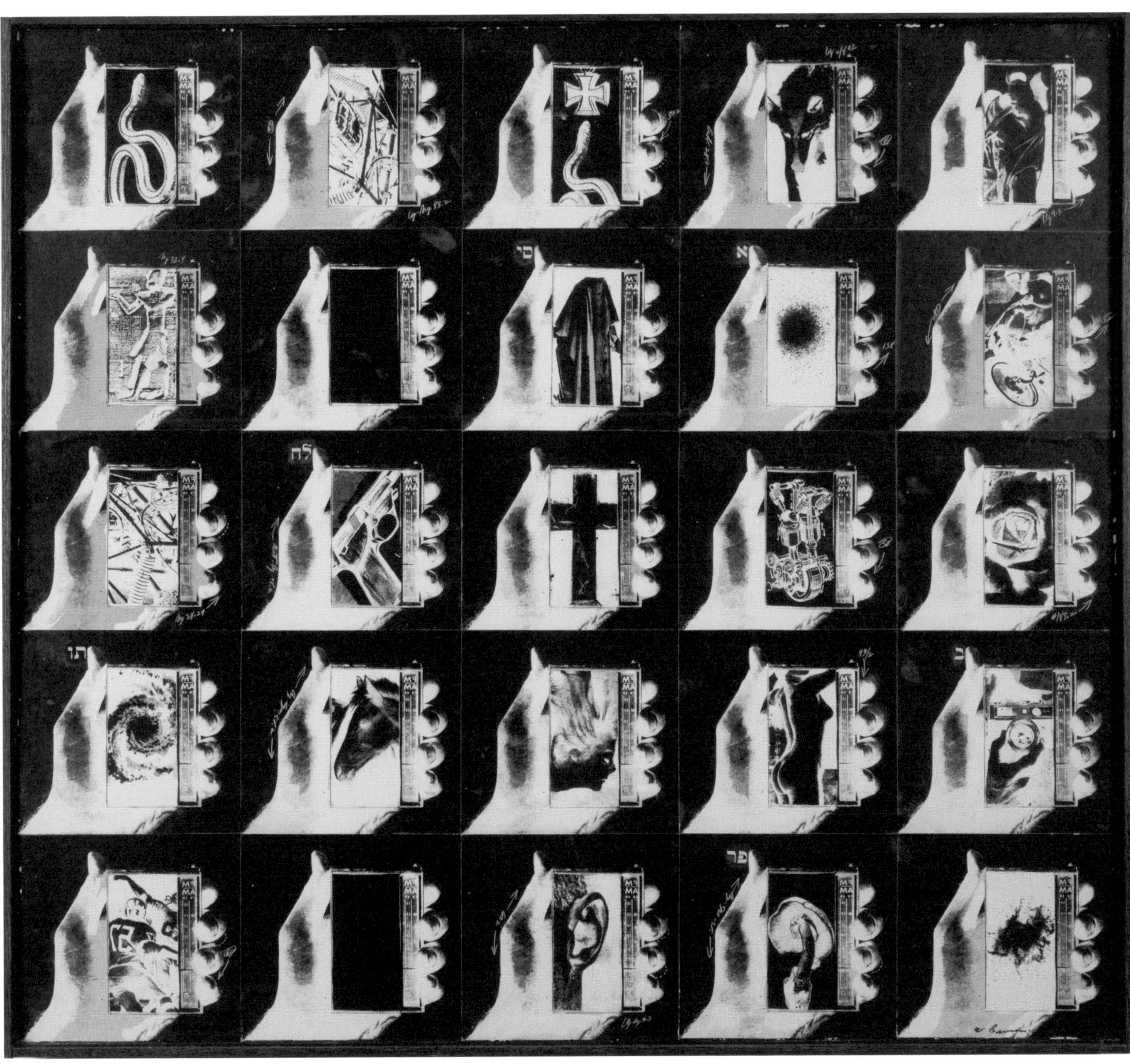

Untitled #129, 1976
single Verifax collage with acrylic
6 × 6.5 inches (15.25 × 16.5 cm)

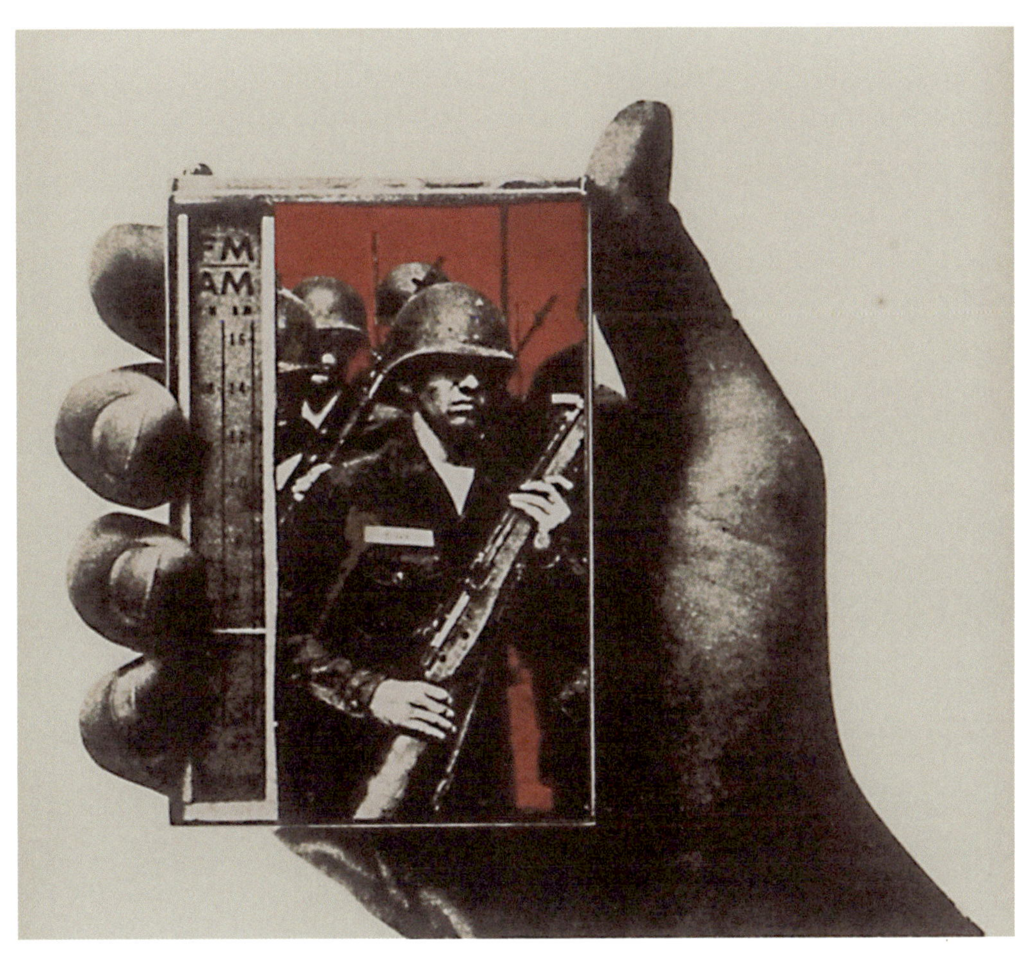
FM
AM

Untitled #125, c. 1964–76
single Verifax collage with acrylic
6 × 6.5 inches (15.25 × 16.5 cm)

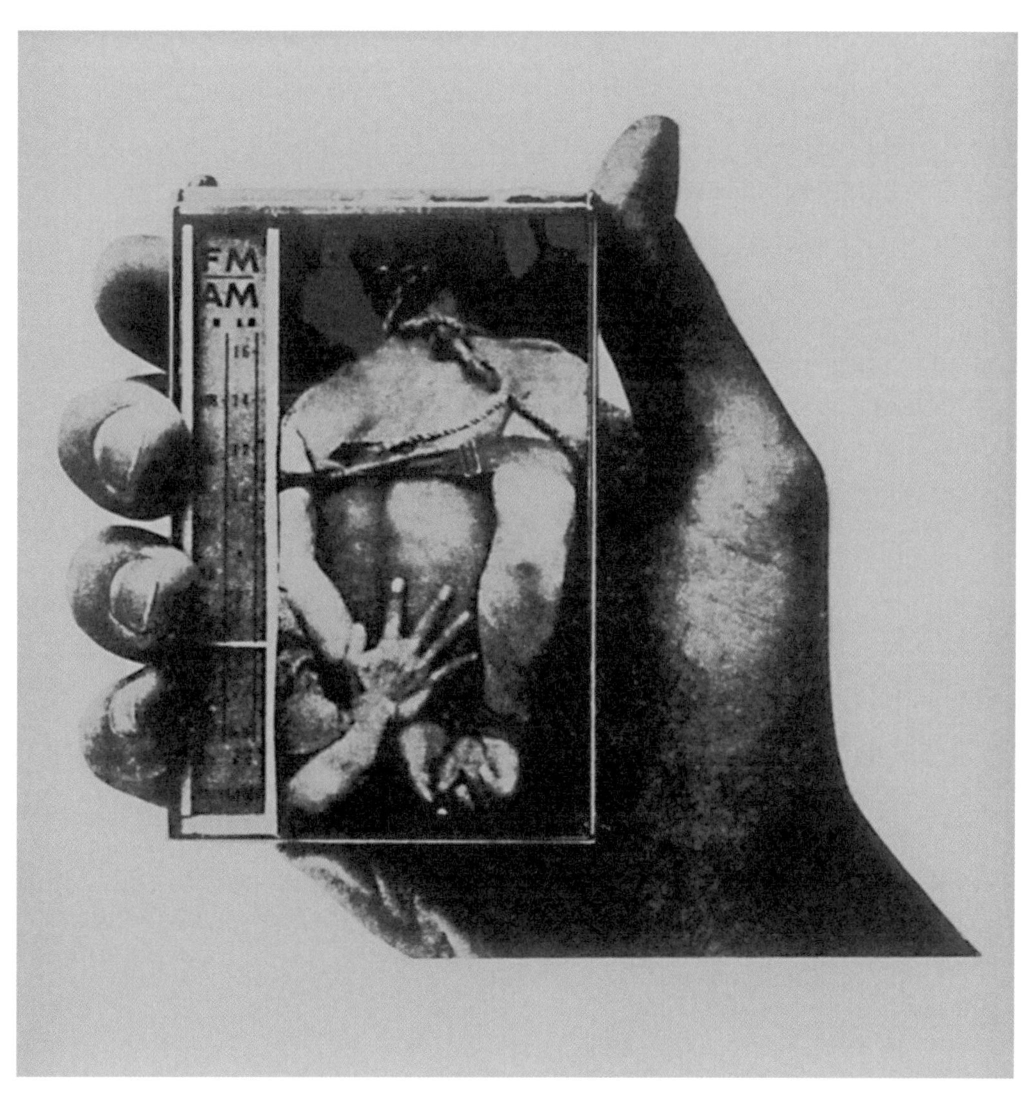
FM
AM

Untitled #126, c. 1964–76
single Verifax collage with acrylic
6 × 6.5 inches (15.25 × 16.5 cm)

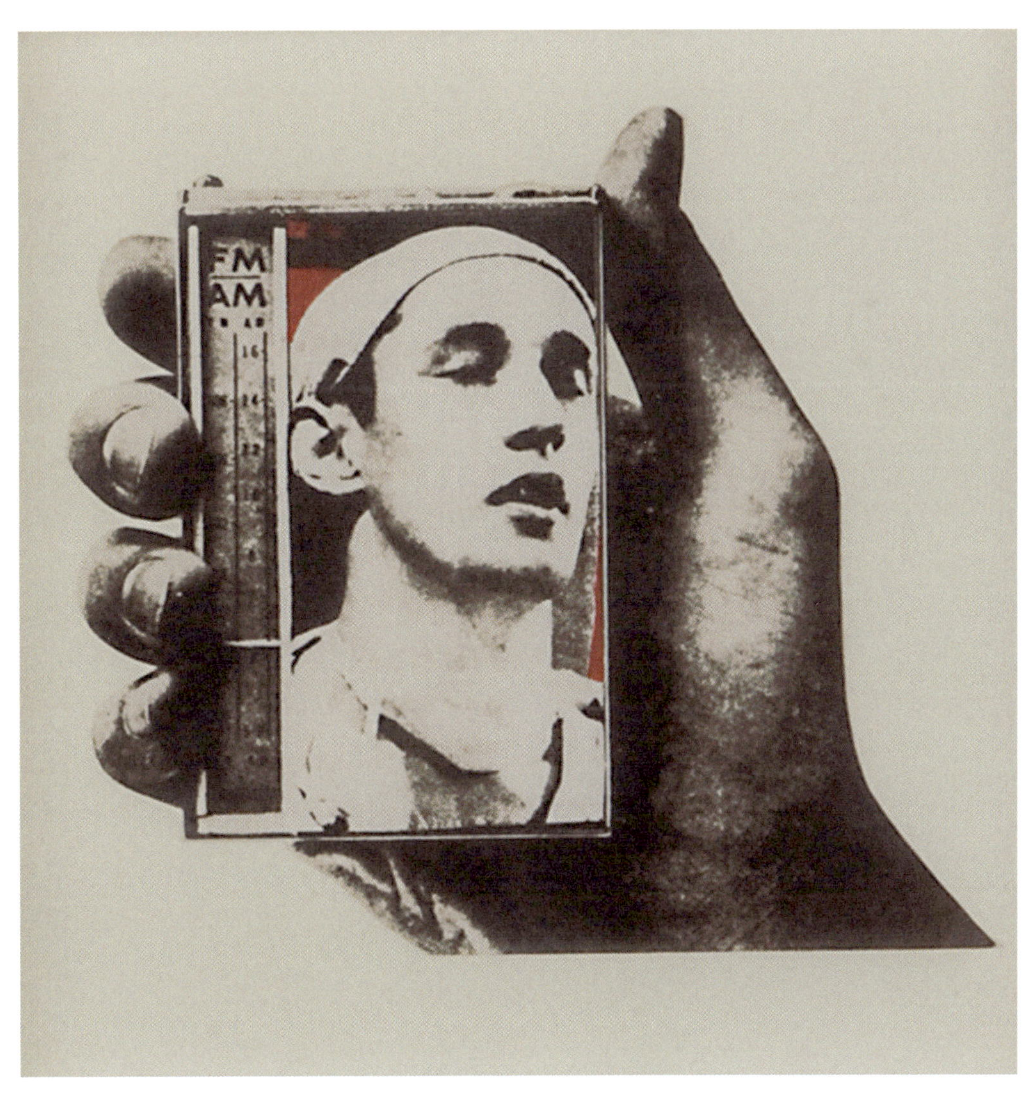
FM
AM

Untitled #120, c. 1964–76
single negative Verifax collage
6 × 6.5 inches (15 × 16.5 cm)

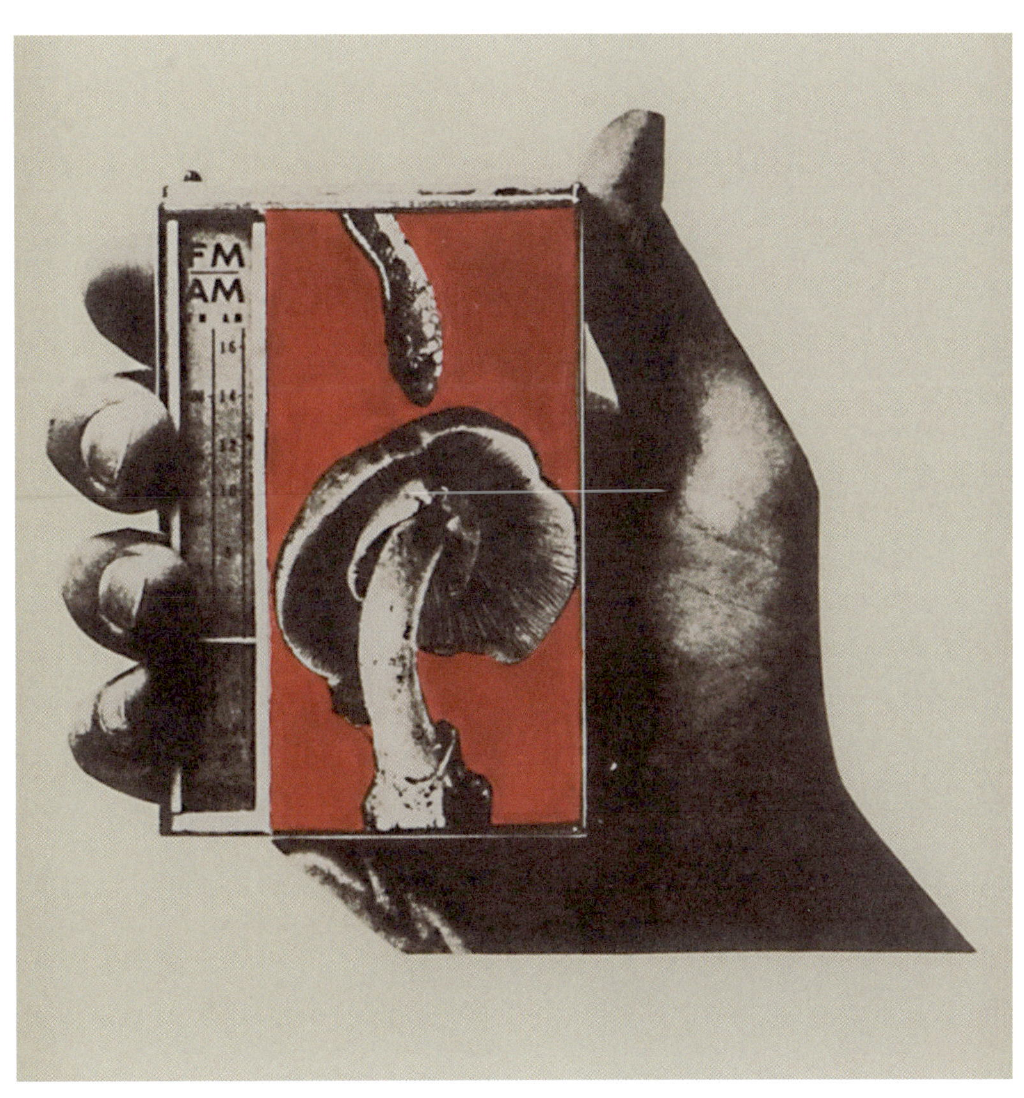
FM
AM

Untitled (Faceless Faces with Kabbalah), 1963
paint on photograph mounted on board with hand-applied varnish
34 × 30 inches (86.5 × 76 cm)

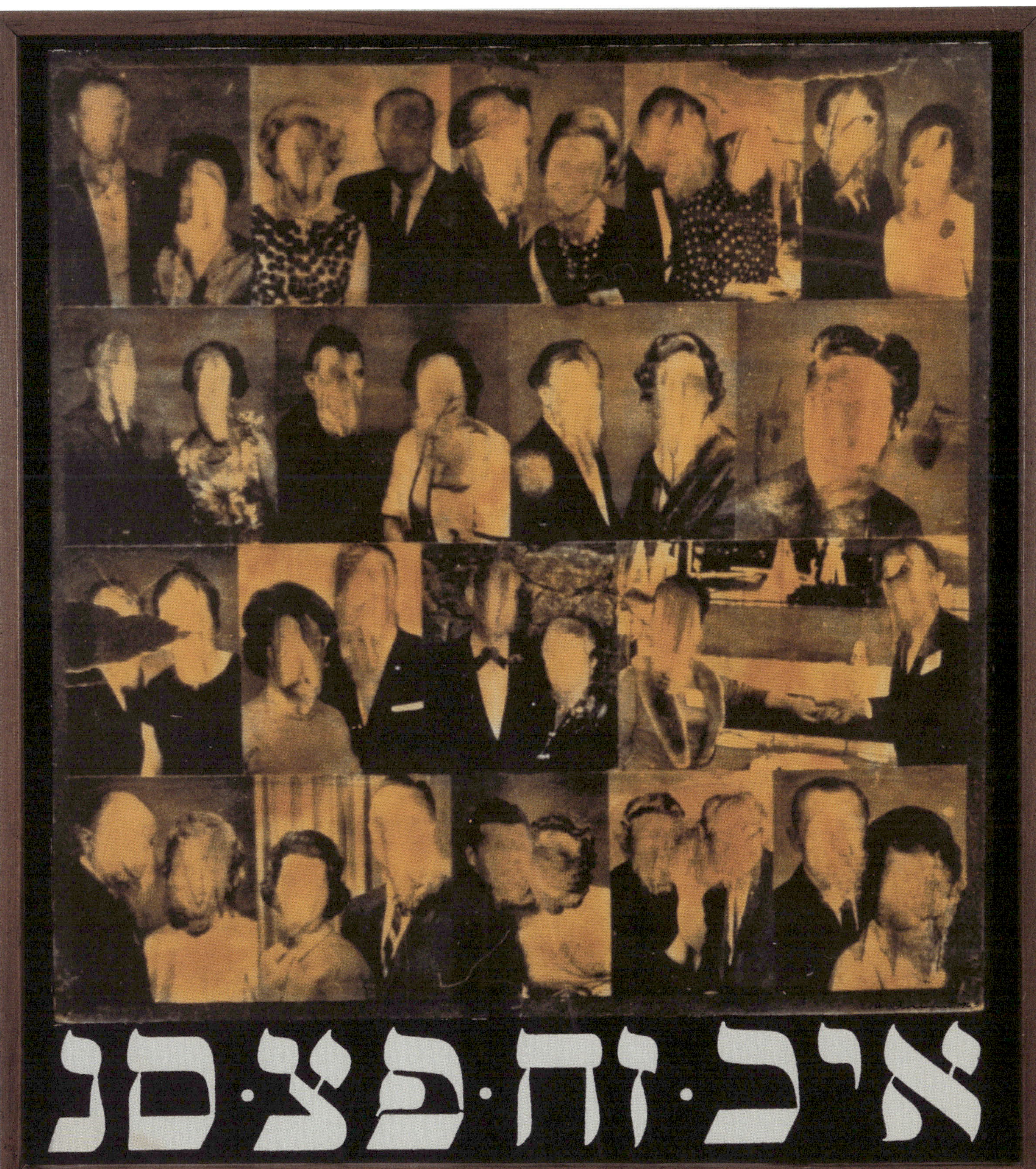

איכ·זח·פצ·סנ

Untitled (Office Management), 1964
Verifax collage on book page
10 × 7.75 inches (25.5 × 19.5 cm)

and performs other miscellaneous work. Functionalization, however, is to [illegible] fullest extent only feasible in large offices. It is uneconomical to have too many department[illegible] one officer. A chart of the organization, a[illegible] gram, both giving not only the position of [illegible] the office but his duties and relation to other[illegible]. Also there should be standard methods for pe[illegible] and written standard practice instructions so th[illegible] methods may be perpetuated. Otherwise [illegible] result.

Personnel Methods.—Progressive [illegible] performance are necessary as t[illegible] advancement. Special tests fo[illegible] cert[illegible] of new employees will prevent to a [illegible] ex[illegible] gr[illegible] wastage of continuous hiring and discha[illegible]. [illegible] psychological special ability and trade tests [illegible] prepared [illegible] used and found advantageous. [illegible] PSYCHOLOG[illegible] MENT.) While there are many [illegible] positions which [illegible] the very highest intelligence, all c[illegible] work does not, and much of the simpler clerical work is [illegible] to those capable of a higher grade [illegible]. Tr[illegible] emely important, though often sadly neglected. In [illegible] the various lines of promotion are laid down and made [illegible] employees, so they can prepare themselves for ad[illegible]. Some offices also have officers, who devote their acti[illegible]lly to employment, and all persons who are to be di[illegible] are referred for final adjudication to this officer—the em[illegible] manager. [illegible] advantage here is that competent empl[illegible] are not lost to organization solely because of the perso[illegible]ique of som[illegible] or temperamental officer. The employment manager al[illegible] tains by t[illegible] questioning the reasons [illegible] why employees and by a [illegible] classified record of such reasons is [illegible] check ba[illegible]s, and to determine any other causes fo[illegible] faction.

Turn[illegible] "rate of turnover," that is, the ra[illegible] ployees [illegible] to those on the pay roll [illegible] factor in [illegible] office management, [illegible] $100 is represented in the training of a[illegible] one who has left, so that it is evident [illegible]yees for long periods. Turnover [illegible]s. If employees are not prop[illegible] select[illegible] will be needed; if salaries are [illegible] or the relations of officers [illegible] she[illegible] voluntary separations. A [illegible] tu[illegible]out 10% annually. Length [illegible] conditions as rate of turn[illegible]

Routines and Metho[illegible] operations through whic[illegible] Divis[illegible] labour has [illegible] few [illegible] are seldom co[illegible] ally through the use o[illegible] As a result, operations w[illegible] no value to the "finished [illegible] quently found. Methods [illegible] evolution, and yield great result[illegible] both routines and methods are [illegible] be r[illegible] waste.

C[illegible] **Output.**—T[illegible] mu[illegible] sar[illegible] wo[illegible] ca[illegible] of [illegible] of similar character [illegible] the office there is the added difficulty that office work [illegible]ilar character does not always take the same course; and even in some work of exactly the same nature, the flow is governed by conditions beyond the control of the office manager. Because of this fact it was, until very recently, considered impossible to plan and schedule office work. Peaks, that is, periods demanding intensified and additional work, were handled either by overtime work, or by the permanent maintenance of a sufficient force of clerks to handle them, both plans being evidently wasteful. Analysis of this matter, however, showed that in many cases they could [illegible] pre-planning. The office force should be [illegible] sufficiently large to handle average condition[illegible]ber of clerks should be trained in several ope[illegible] utilizing the idea of the "flying squadron"—[illegible] of clerks that can be used almost anywhere [illegible]—most of the minor peaks can be handled wi[illegible]. Major peaks can be dealt with by a re-adjustm[illegible] force and the employment of extra clerks for [illegible] require only a minimum of training.

Clerica[illegible] **Ou**[illegible]n this subject all the major factors of office ma[illegible]rge, and all have a bearing upon it. Under conditio[illegible] factors have been scientifically studied, clerical [illegible]ably much greater than in organizations in whi[illegible]y ignored. Thus in the office of the latter chara[illegible] output of a stenographer will rarely exceed 100 sq.in. [illegible] while in a scientifically managed office this particular [illegible] be increased to an average of 200 sq.in. per hour. [illegible]enance of the latter rate does not depend alone [illegible] and application of the stenographer—for [illegible] but 30 words a minute, while the world's [illegible] over 800 sq.in. per hour—but largely upon [illegible] the control of the operator and decidedly [illegible] office manager. As with typewriting, so it is [illegible] clerical operations; the output usually depends [illegible] the efforts [illegible]agement than upon those [illegible] clerk. The effort should not be to obtain the [illegible]utput from an[illegible] individual, but that which [illegible] from a first-class worker.

[illegible]**ge.**—Still another factor which aids in ob[illegible]tput is an incentive wage of some kind, [illegible] measure the wor[illegible]. The various methods [illegible]n other lines of business endeavour have [illegible]ce, some with considerable success, others [illegible]s. In the cases of failure the main causes generally a[illegible] work was not properly standardized; (2) not pr[illegible]d; (3) steady flow not obtained; (4) work not pr[illegible]lled; and (5) no adequate check upon its quality. [illegible] in the office is not so generally applicable, because [illegible] must have a guaranteed minimum wage, and it is [illegible]ssible to supply him with sufficient work to ma[illegible] on a piece-work basis.

THE MECHANICAL SIDE

The [illegible]g factors deal almost wholly with the management [illegible] element, and now other factors must be considered—[illegible] factors without which efficient management is not [illegible]

[illegible]**nt.**—The physical arrangement of an office affects [illegible]rs [illegible] management. As most offices are in large [illegible]re high and therefore space must be conserved. [illegible] the cubicles of the old-fashioned office are giving [illegible]ce. Departments having relations with each [illegible] contiguously situated and the seating of the [illegible]rtment be regulated also on this principle. [illegible] straight lines. Adequate light, both daylight [illegible] provided, the standard of the latter being [illegible] not less than [illegible]-candles. (*See* ILLUMINAT[illegible] The complete indirect system, in which [illegible] from its source to the ceiling, and thence [illegible]sidered the best. Ventilation is an important [illegible] shows [illegible] the best ventilating system [illegible] fresh [illegible] the outside without altering [illegible] the elaborate washed and heated air systems. [illegible]D VENTILATION.) Excessive noise is also detrimental to good work, and noisy machines, if numerous, should be segregated.

Equipment.—Under this head are included desks, tables, chairs, filing cabinets and similar furnishings. The old-fashioned roll-top desk has disappeared, and as the present tend-

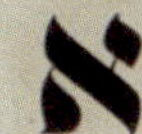

Untitled (A1-Jet), 1964–76
Four-part positive Verifax collage
13 × 14 inches (33 × 35.5 cm)

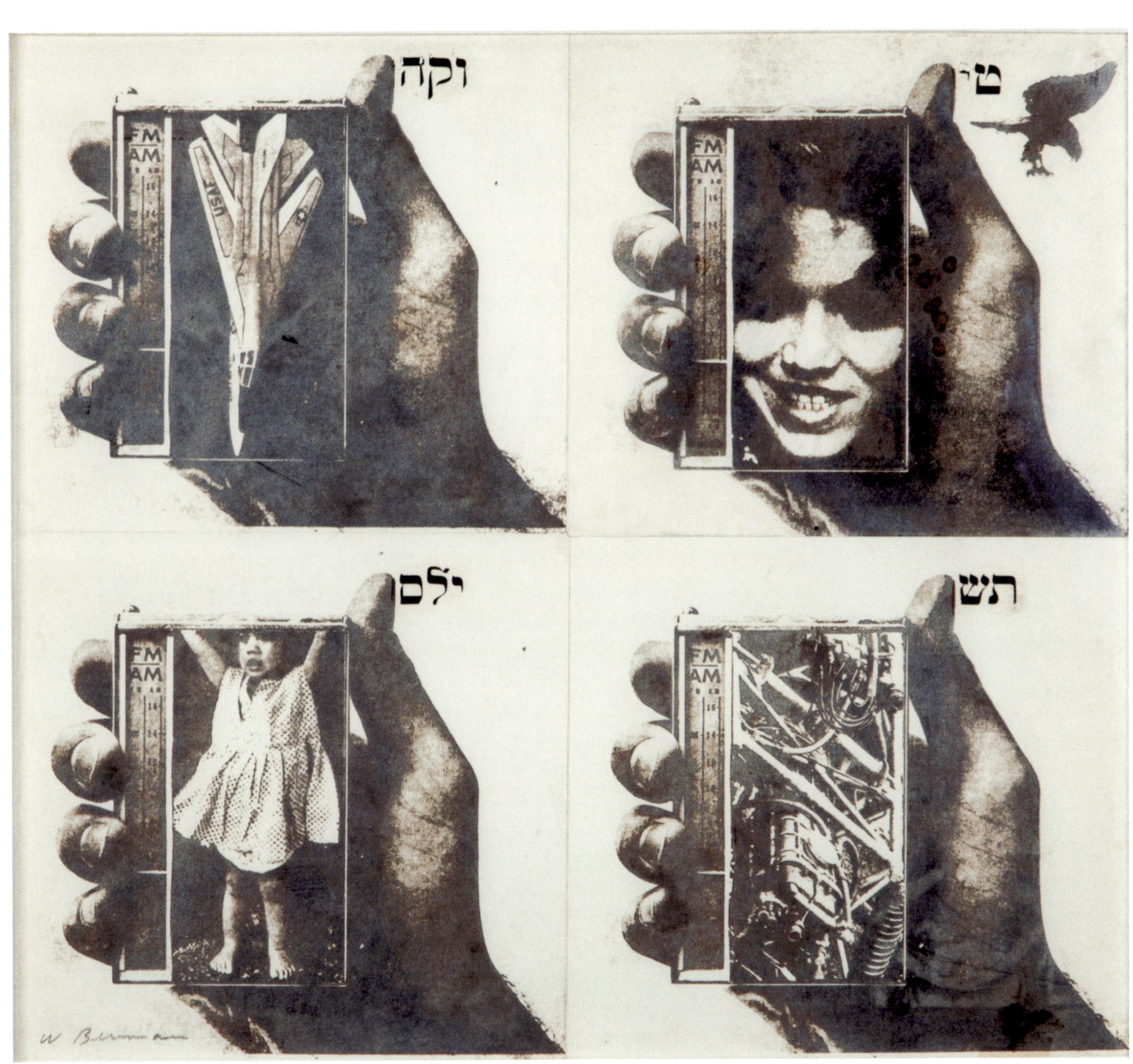

וקה
FM
AM
USAF
טי
FM
AM
ילם
FM
AM
תש
FM
AM

Untitled (A1-Nebulae), 1964–76
Four-part negative Verifax collage
13 × 14 inches (33 × 35.5 cm)

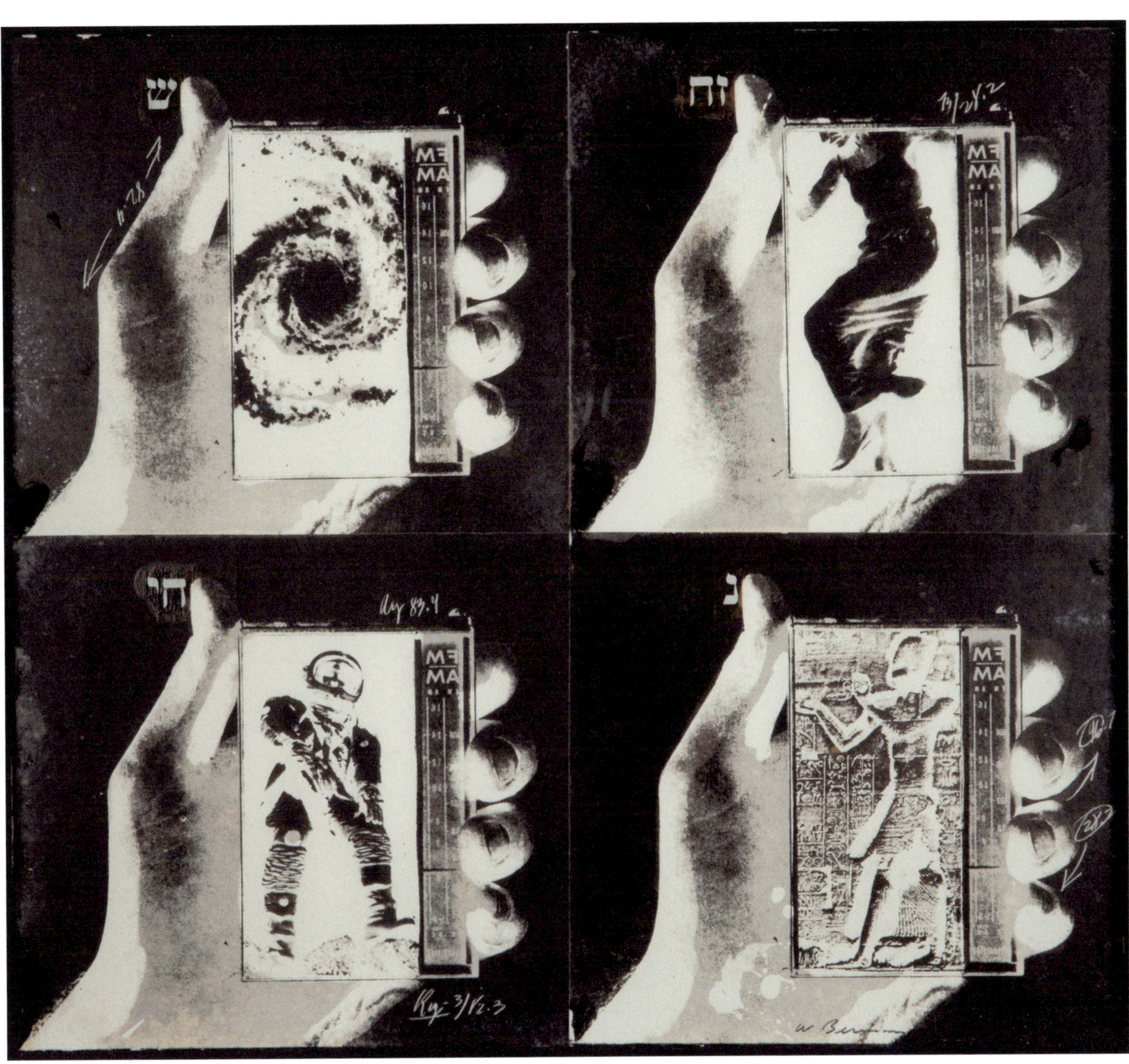

ש
זח

Untitled, 1964–76
Four-part negative Verifax collage
13 × 14 inches (33 × 35.5 cm)

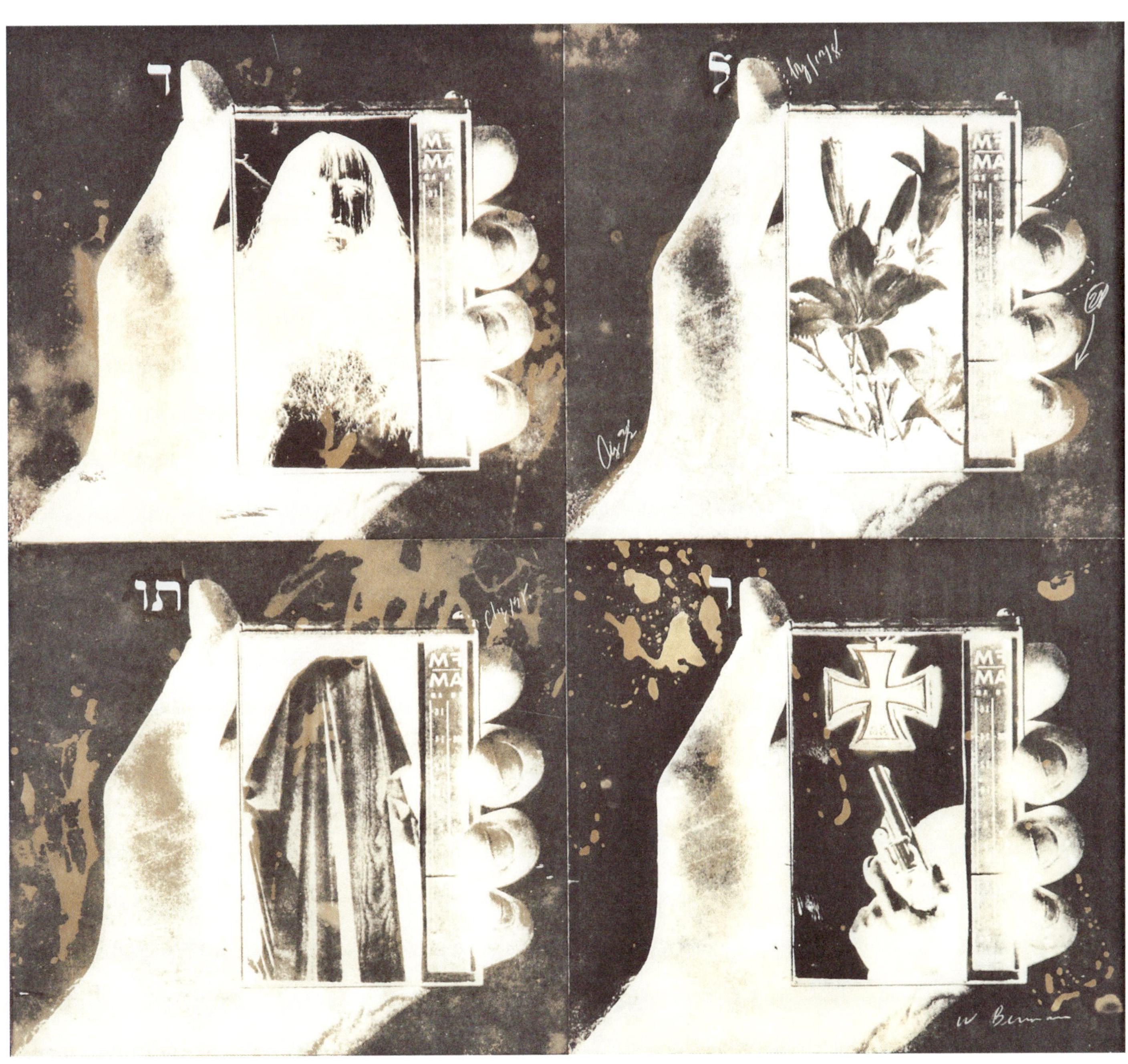

Untitled, 1964–76
Four-part positive Verifax collage
13 × 14 inches (33 × 35.5 cm)

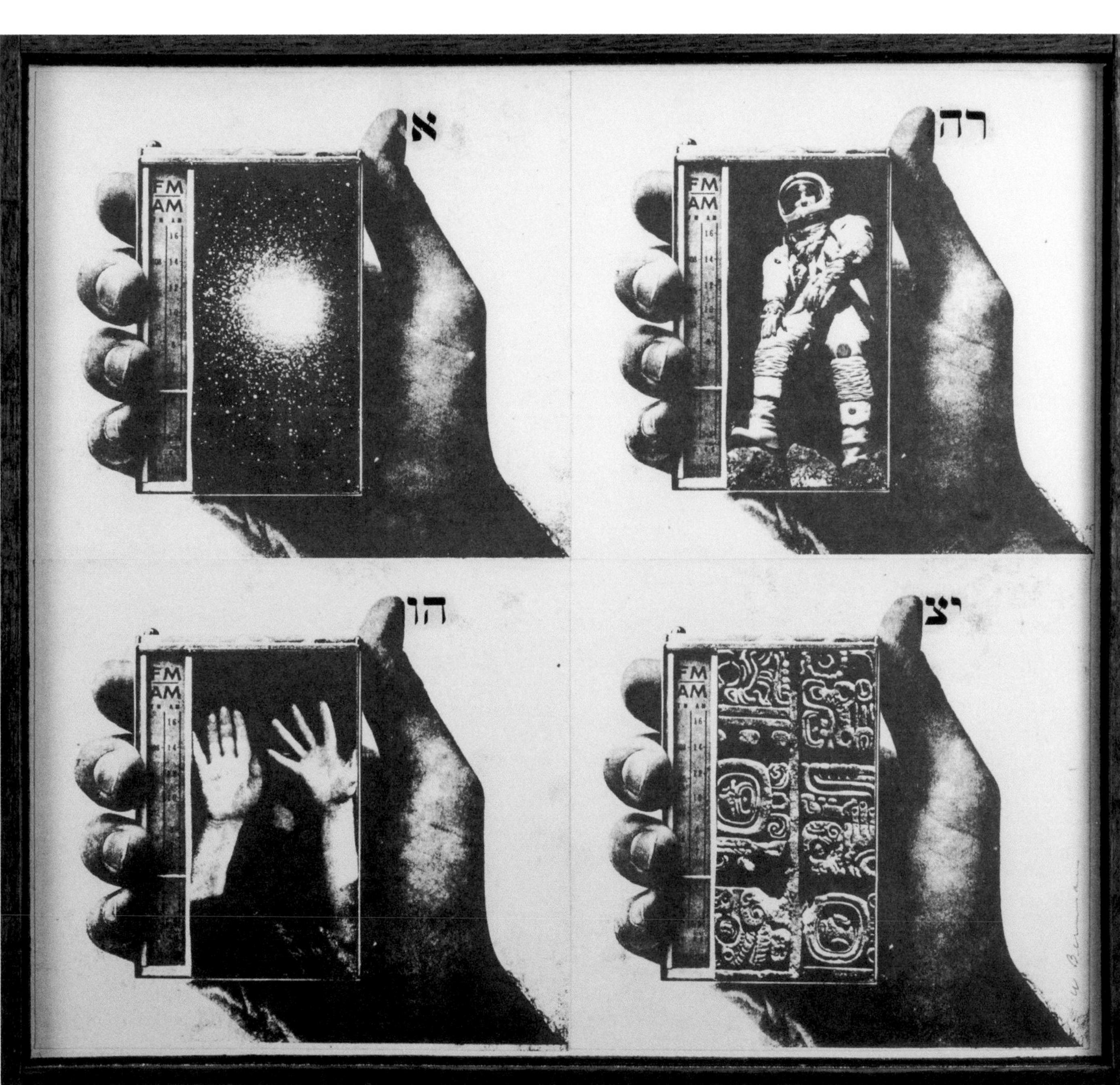
א
FM
AM
רה
FM
AM
הו
FM
AM
יצ
FM
AM

Untitled, 1956–57
woodstain and ink on parchment on canvas
19.5 × 19.5 inches (49.5 × 49.5 cm)

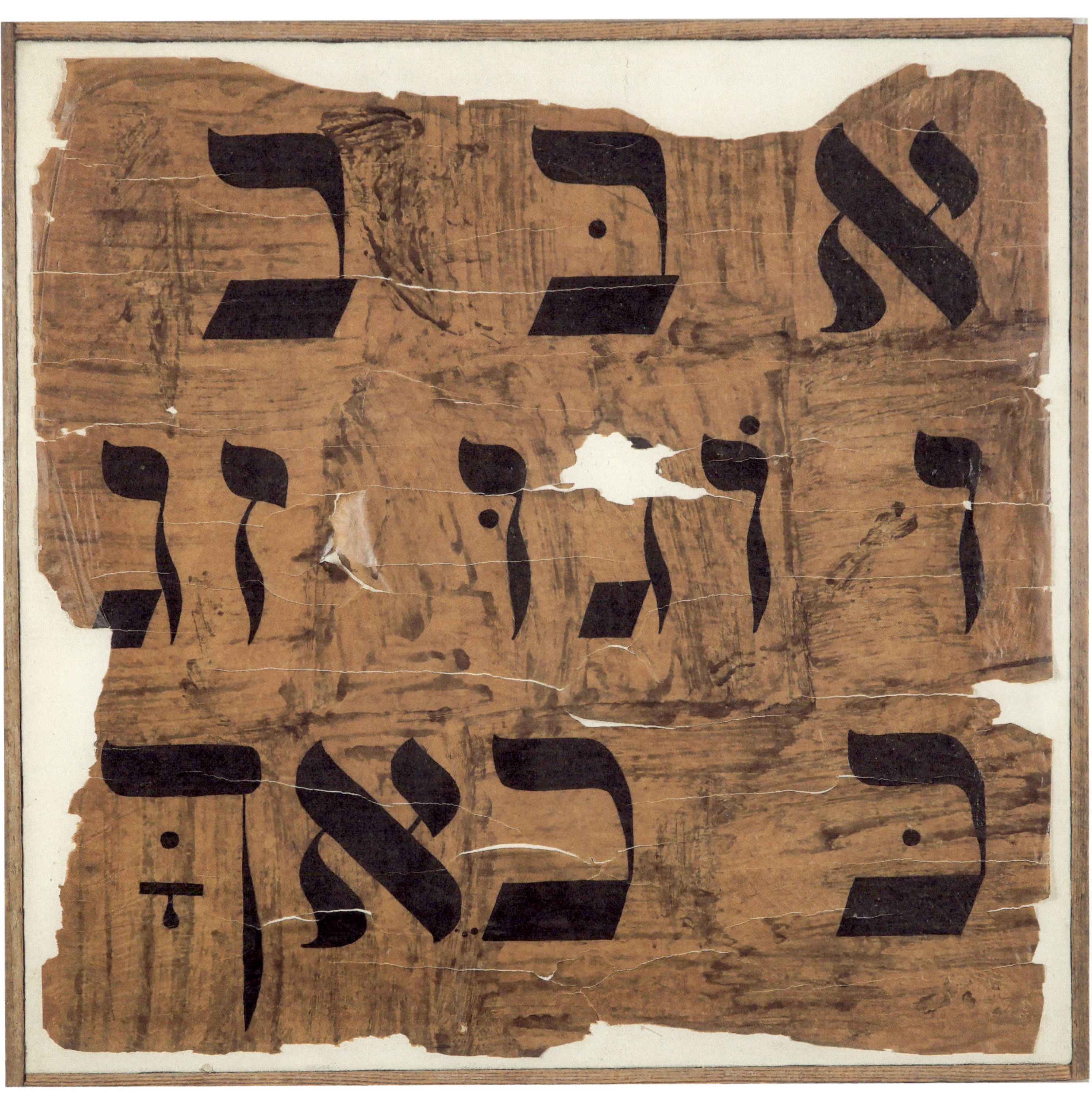

Untitled (Odd Couple Red Background), 1970
collage
6.25 × 5 inches (16 × 13 cm)

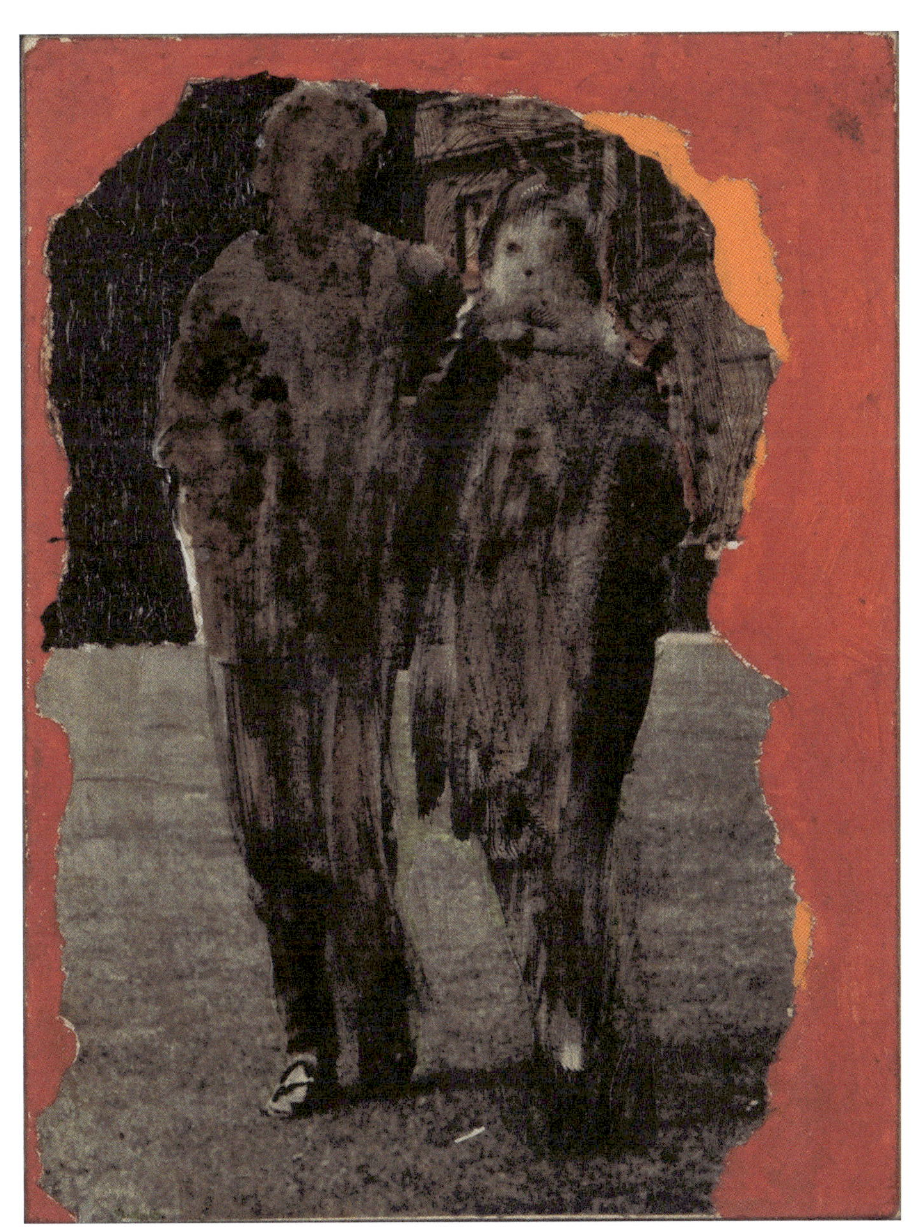

Untitled (Jack Ruby), 1964
photograph with handwritten poem
28.5 × 29 inches (72.5 × 73.5 cm)

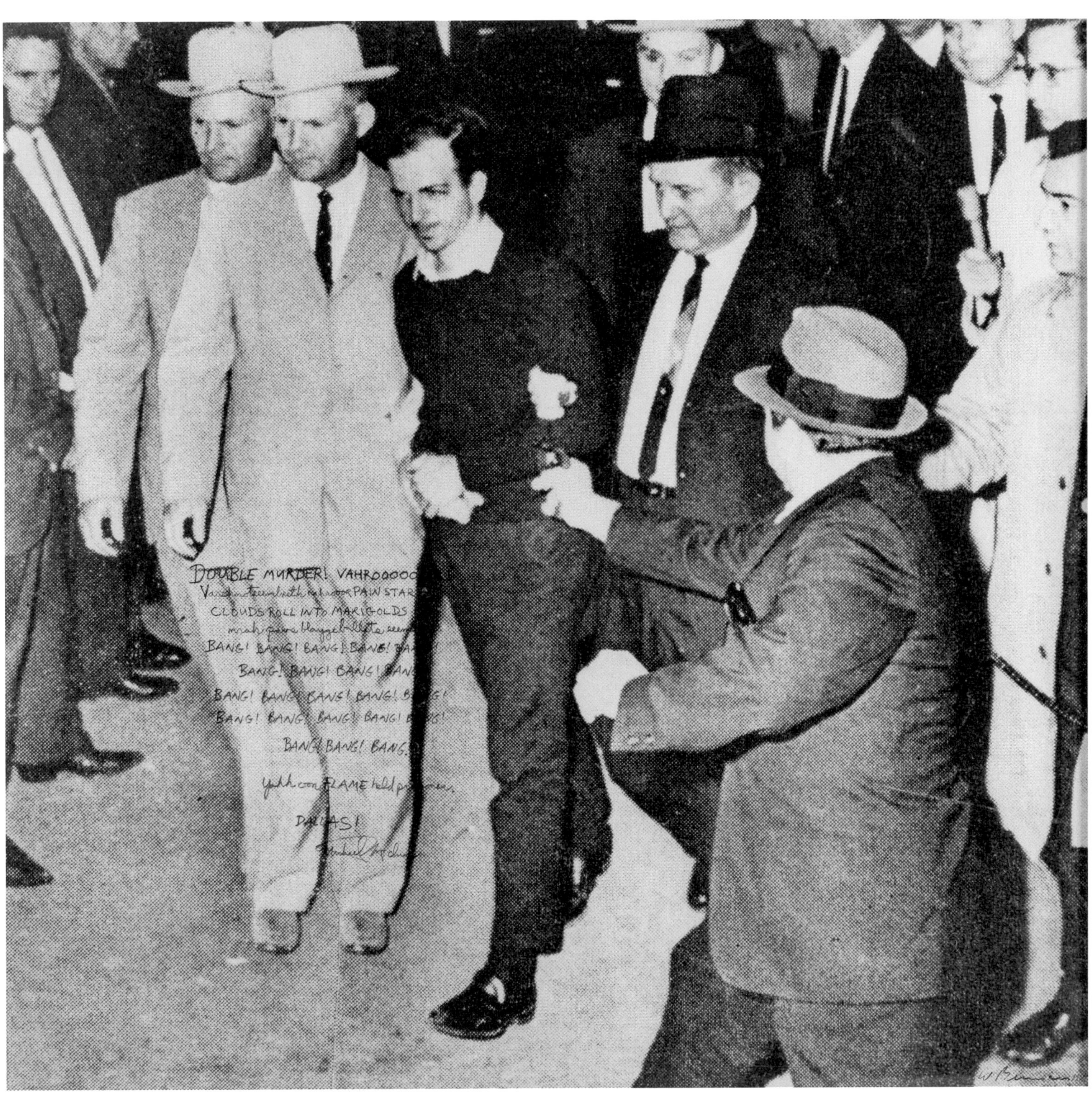
DOUBLE MURDER! VAHROOOOO
CLOUDS ROLL INTO MARIGOLDS
BANG! BANG! BANG!
BANG! BANG! BANG!
BANG! BANG! BANG! BANG!
BANG! BANG! BANG! BANG!
BANG! BANG! BANG
FLAME

Untitled (Insert in "Semina" 7), 1961
offset lithograph from the *Semina* facsimile
4.75 × 3.75 inches (12 × 9.5 cm)

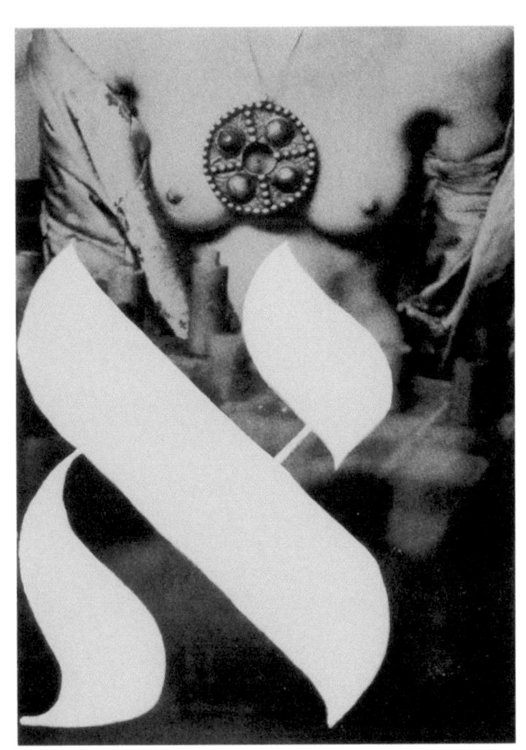
א

SCRY TOWARD AUGURY

by ANNE WALDMAN

in response to
Wallace Berman: Off the Grid
at TOTAH, New York, October 2021

"The machines are too dull when we are lion-poems that move & breathe."
—Michael McLure, *Ghost Tantras*

look into

restructure of cinema

all systems
as you discern
an "unthinkable space"

VAH ROOOO cosmology

hold up
hands as architects of MOURNING & SONG

of mirrors
of nests, of transistors

for one who invented a grid to flow upon
others come after

opposable thumbs; all the icons, rippling
\
building into the antinomian lines of all your palms
bodhisattvas of craft and poetry and silver screen

as blowing and inhaling the studio light

may all trips to the moon make us wiser!

the opposing autocracy of brain is lunacy

while coming to head of the

proverbial

rhythm is the tune
daring collagist!

a form preceding itself as with jazz

an increment all the time within
borders
interstices you
make mark
within a heart upon
masterful in space: divination

Berman's gaze
cuts like spiraling arrows

& with last night's heartbeat

the magic carpet takes off

Ukaz, near Mecca

if you be truly magic

and swear an oath of fealty to the third eye

both vulnerable and strange—look again

into that mirror: ten dimensions

Nureyev in the dream
Michael McClure scribing double murders
inside his poem

& round the gallery there you go

Ezra Pound standing by his word, old ghost

   a ritual, oracle

in ceremony, witnesses

are you undocumented, o artist?

what hand made thee start the clock?

what makes your poem tick?

your work lies stellar

                    what have we gone to invent here in this

drip of grid?

rip of the grip, tide of a whip, Mick Jagger mouthing

the ripe pride, the grinning pride
the gridiron

locked
into a sharp edge of procedure
& I would be a Bedouin on that assignment

inside the tribe

Hollywood's odd angel

on promise, & illusion

let's go to the bar place

in the desert

take a handle on the rope that holds your camel

keep her terrestrial—

a long march
   a watch of night
   and what sounds are heard

artist in his cave?

a round of entanglements
in the minimalist academy
   Hebrew letters aflame

disentangle your threads,
spooky at a distance
let's go the distance

what better way to leave a trace
but why must one die so young?

into tantra's memory way back
to disappear in a burst of

crystal flesh

YOU ARE WAVING AND HOLDING
&
PUTTING HAND UP TO AIR
OVER A HEAD AS YOU SPIN

pointing to Sufi clouds

Dharmakaya spins under stress of work
& love, then goes blank like bliss

pointing at a first letter, first word, Aleph

what is blocked, what secret inner lifeline
   to this twenty-first century's collapse

why does the mark

come of rubble?

   screens that hold you fast
toxic, the brain

SUFI starting to spin OUR TIME
      AS ALCHEMIST
warning

"to wise up the marks"

an elegant wood stain, a craft beside itself
a beauty of alignment

what is nebula to a black hole?
nudity

do they coexist?

flog a moonstone?

make a heaven for mothers,
                of eternal return?

Shirley, the sylph, her memory of all this

a revolutionary event, human, seminal

turning a delicate hand toward Tosh

MAKE THE SCREEN COME MARVELOUSLY
HUMANIZED
AND HOLD THE MIRROR UP TO ITS NATURE
     A SYMBOL OF HANDS ACROSS THE HEART
(of a child)

William Burroughs crossed this galaxy

Allen Ginsberg could admire the wild

Diane di Prima embraced the liberated Kabbalah

do we perform this work, scry our eyes out

looking for salvation or risk?

and bounce off the screens of imposter life?

the dictator still in the airbrush
& we in our sacred niches

PARCHMENT WILL BE
EMBOLDENED THRU ETERNAL TIME
and the celluloid rolls on

THE LONG PATH OR THE SHORT?

enigmas of origins fold back on themselves

and you look into the palm of space on the other side of
time: toreador, lily, astronaut, rune, Buddha
hands and ears reach for the sensorium

where you live on in precarity, and we are stuck
with the year of the metal ox
a swirl of deep yearning

end-time of performance
to lift the load
Berman's alchemy
taught us

how simple that leg dances toward the future
through flesh, through brotherhood
through love
I want to see all the lines he saw
follow them down—all turbulent waves

geomancy as sand falls through a hand
& sport is reified through power of motion
Verifax has her own sorrow and shadow

& someone poses in a mode of nod
I scry, I scry
I copy, I copy
making it work

Stan Brakhage's
head gazes down

& then you are in negative space

"retard para," "lunar seed," "evolution," the way we live now, in montage

a conscious desire
to lift off the grid because
you can always tower under the matrix
they – the others – makers – deciders – all challenge

crossroads, Stockwell and Tamblyn

a poetry to cross against itself

a crux for your "other" soulmates

to not be elite

word and artist's image

naming a thought of our time

"prescient"

middle ground

"the crystal ball is cloudy"

where Berman is eternally camping on the line
  when Nietzsche aligned with Dionysus
    & cursed

the Babel of our time

every language speaks its own history

what's in that hand?

  a wet colloidal diffusion transfer

—I love the shrouded things
—more drape to mystery

I love the tech-metal

what is revealed of the hidden
Office Management?

crying out for assistance!

come with your face on

a mushroom will occlude my party dress
and the swerve of any hell to be

a martyr will astound
                                        while a syringe in a mouth complicates the borders
of this mount of sound & image

its "algebra of need"

and a moonscape is not what it used to be

will you enter *das capital* of your own volition?

    hold up your part of the deal?

while Ray Charles is running the keys
and the boxer hooks, jabs, uppercuts

    for mandalas to open

& an icon inscribed in adrenalin
                screams
   "ENTER HERE"

and downstairs: Aleph

the first, the second, the cause of our Art

a word that goes both ways

a leap

an adumbration of cosmic flashes

in a trance

a chance encounter
in your mind
streaming with the augur
taking omen from the flight & cries
of meticulous birds.

Untitled, c. 1965
Nine-part positive Verifax collage
18 × 20 inches (45.75 × 51 cm)

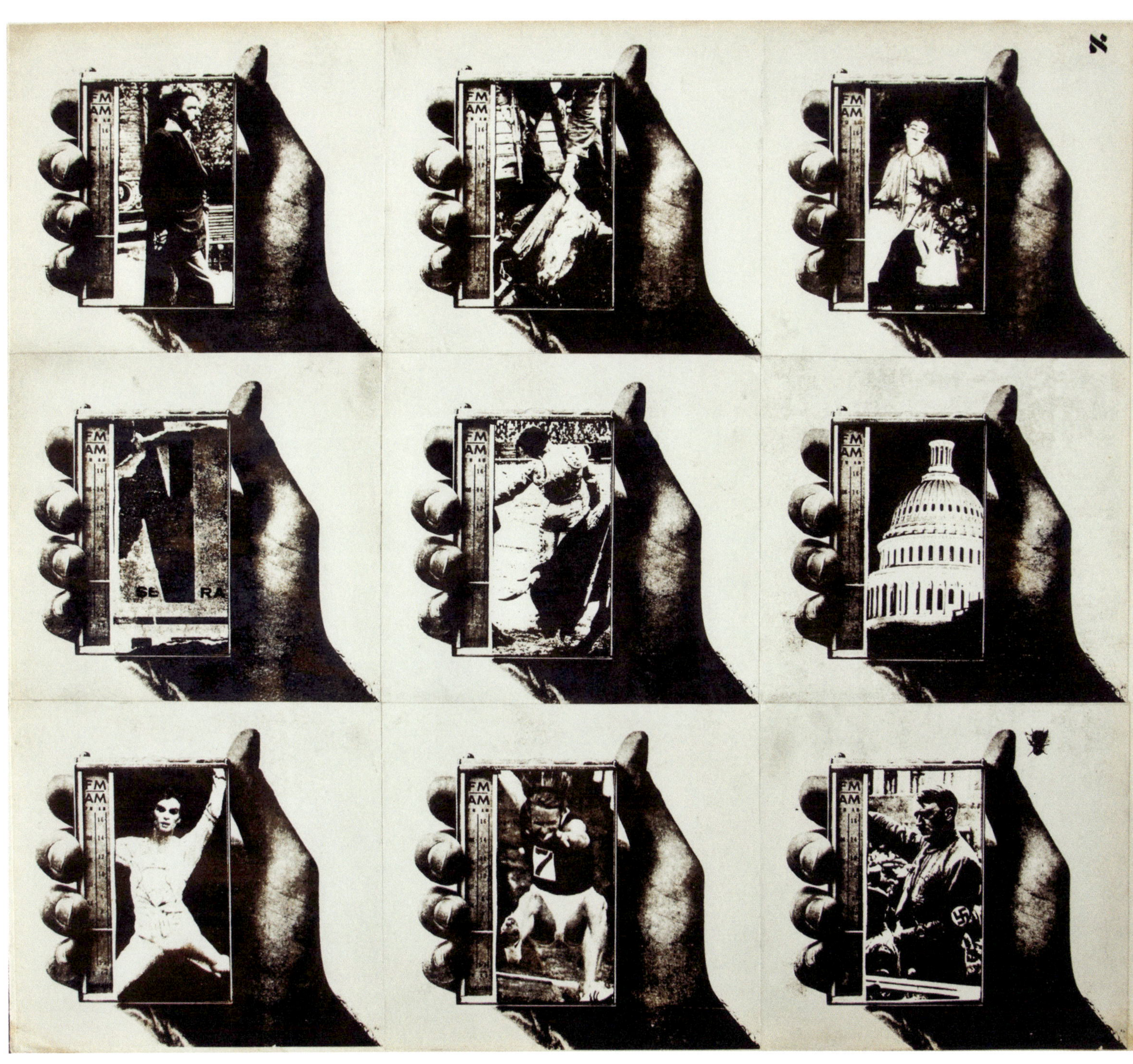
FM
AM

Untitled #58, c. 1964–76
single negative Verifax collage
6 × 6.5 inches (15 × 16.5 cm)

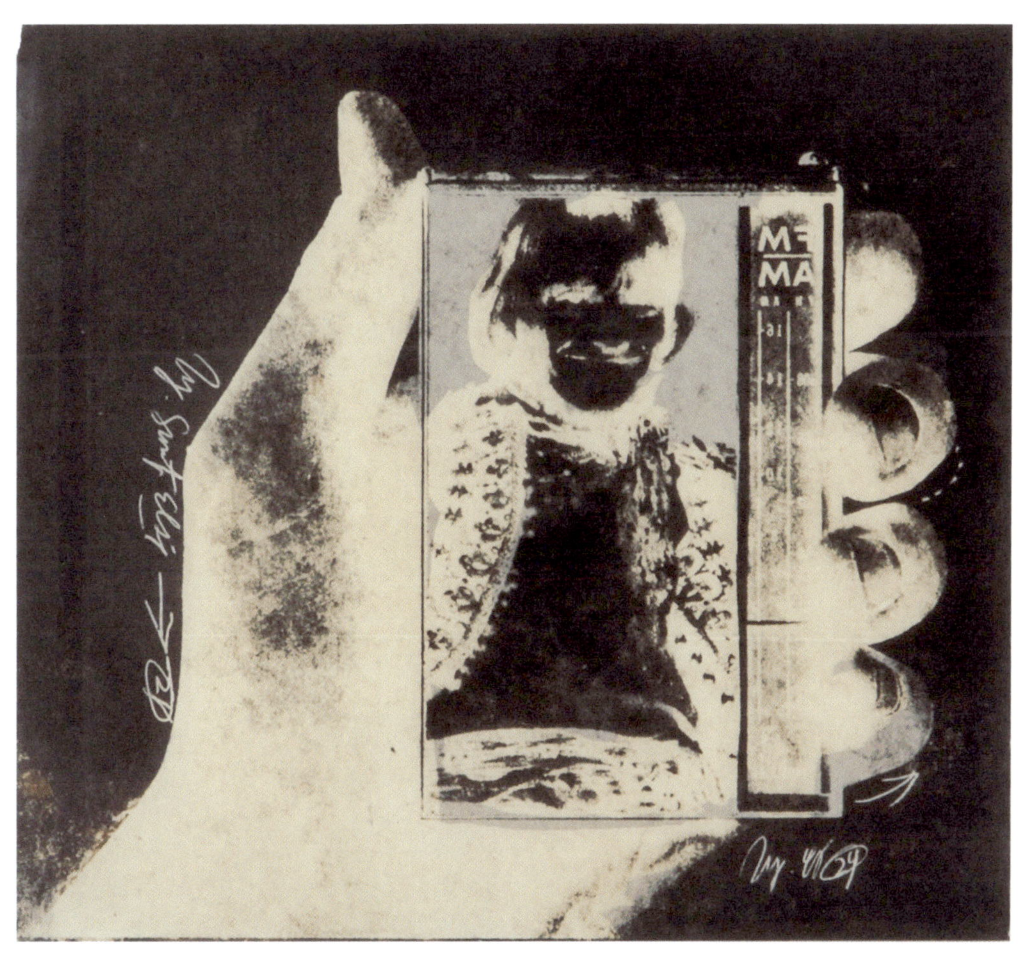

Untitled #128, c. 1964–76
single Verifax collage with acrylic
6 × 6.5 inches (15.25 × 16.5 cm)

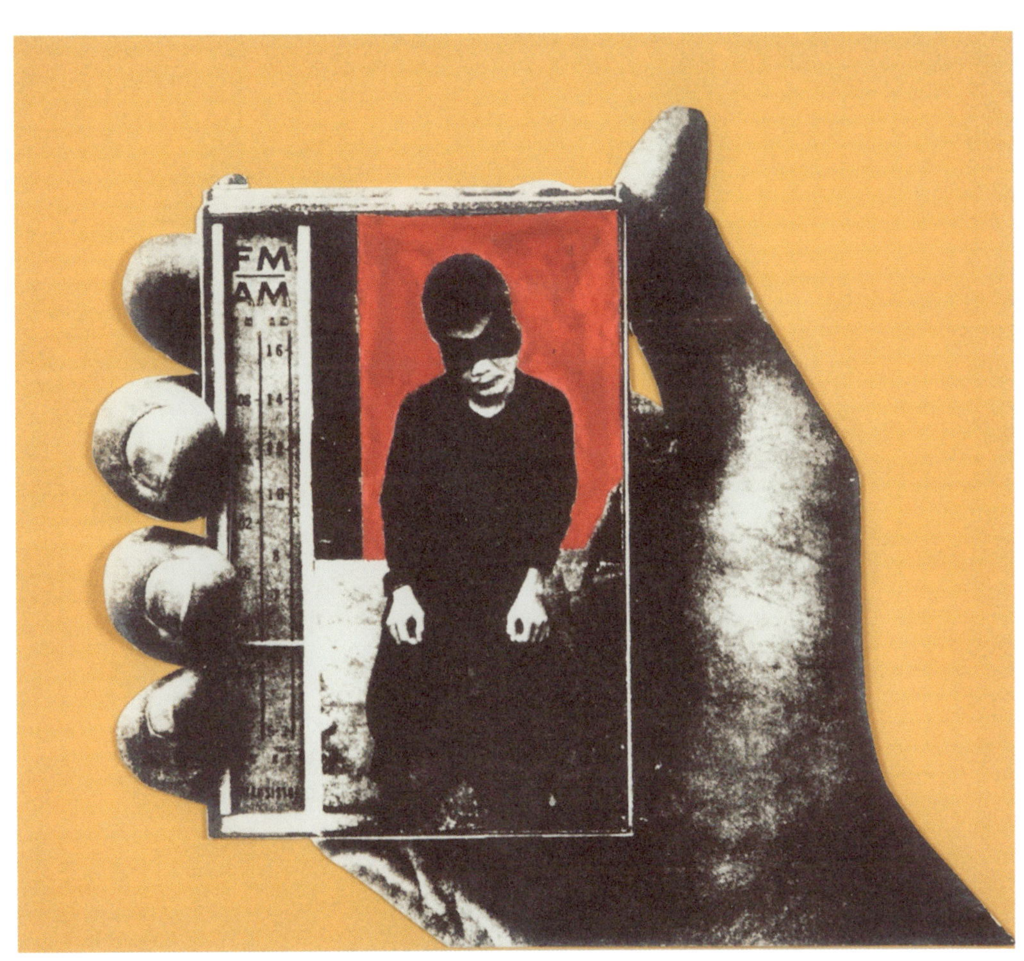
FM
AM

Untitled #82, c. 1964–76
single negative Verifax collage
6 × 6.5 inches (15 × 16.5 cm)

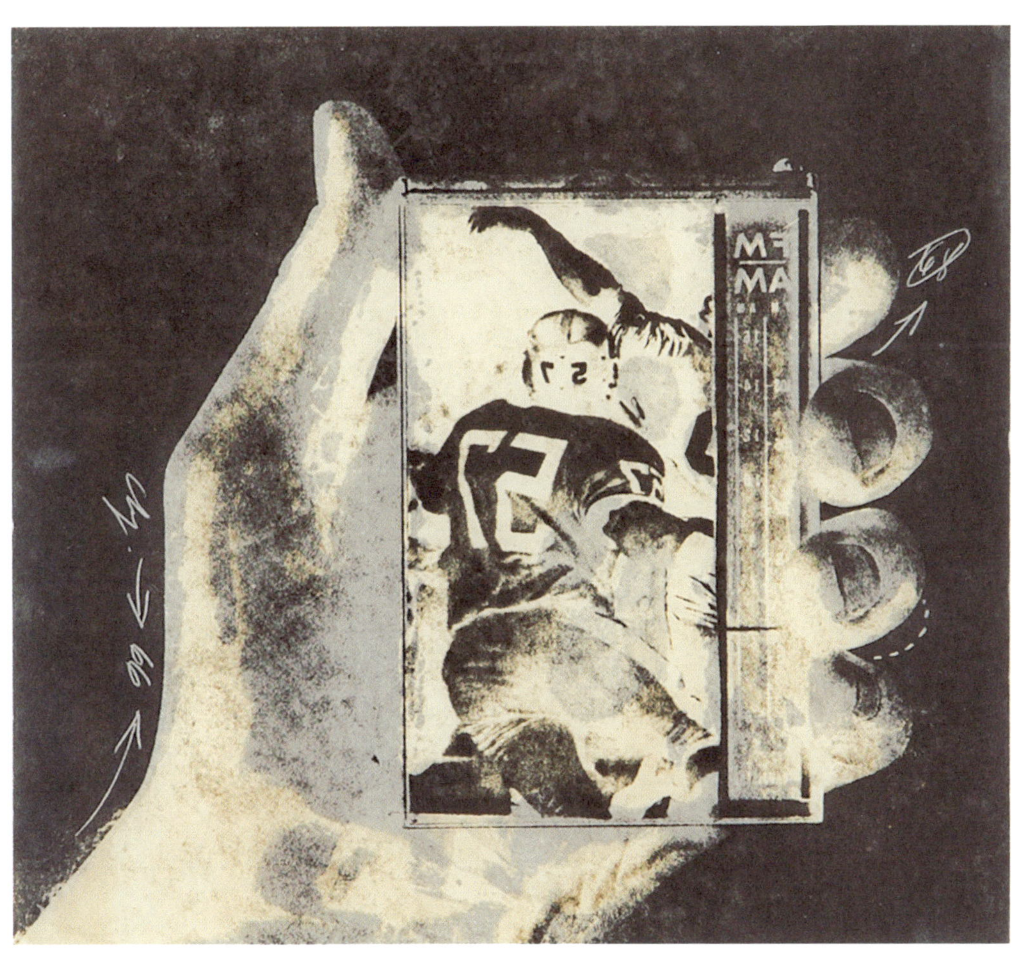

Untitled #109, c. 1964–76
single negative Verifax collage
6 × 6.5 inches (15 × 16.5 cm)

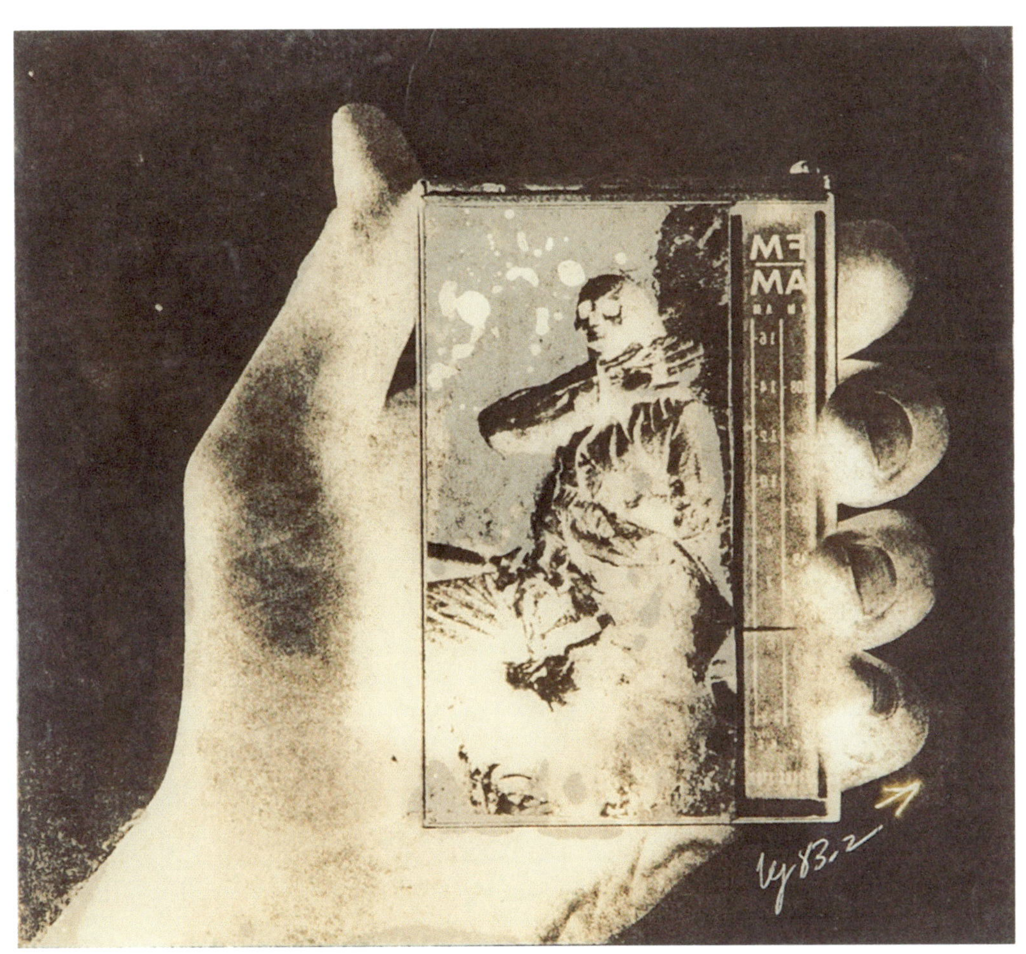

Untitled #102, c. 1964–76
single negative Verifax collage
6 × 6.5 inches (15 × 16.5 cm)

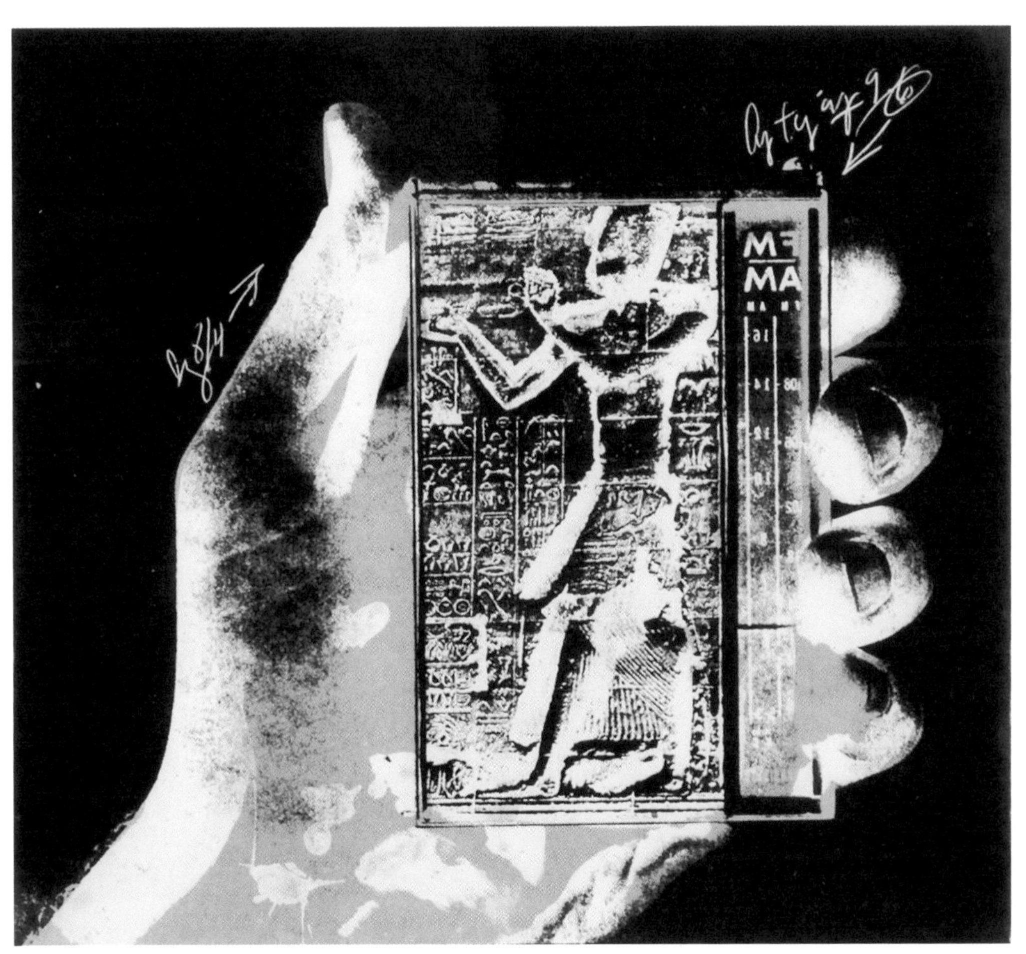

Untitled #21, c. 1964–76
single negative Verifax collage
6 × 6.5 inches (15 × 16.5 cm)

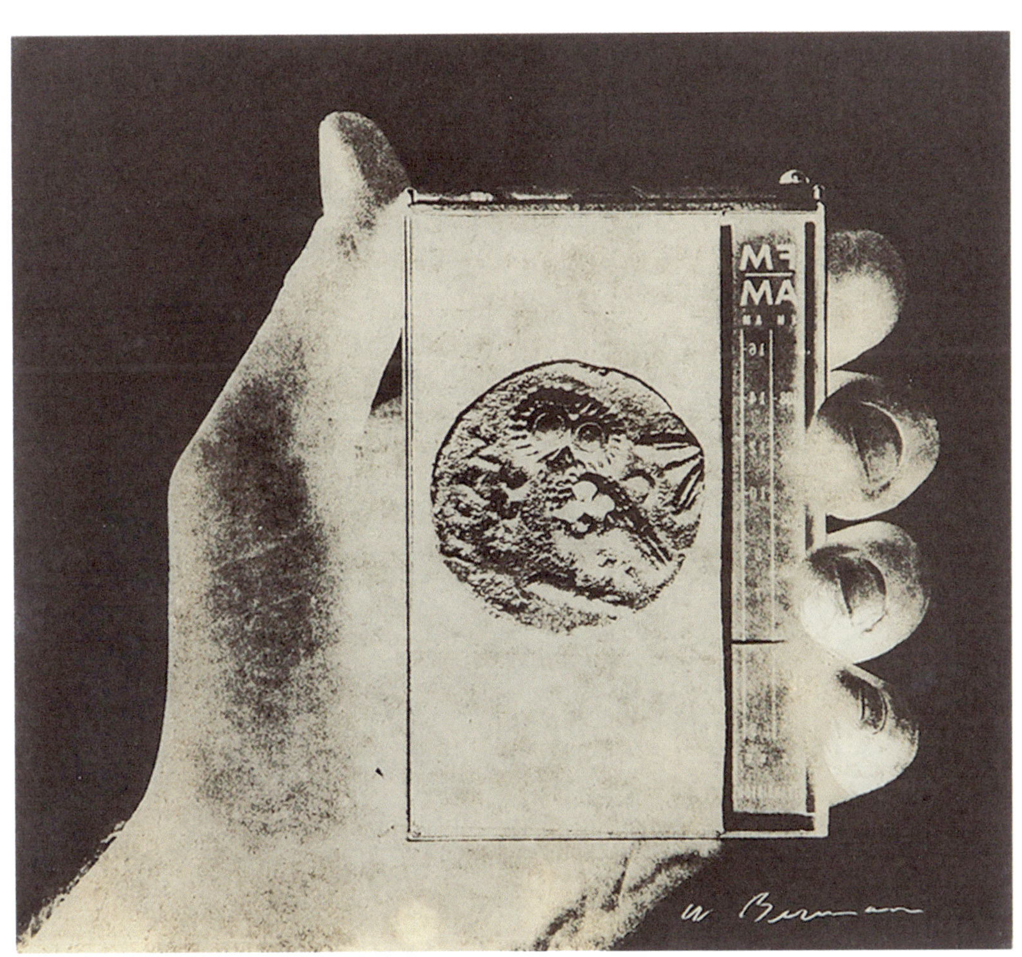

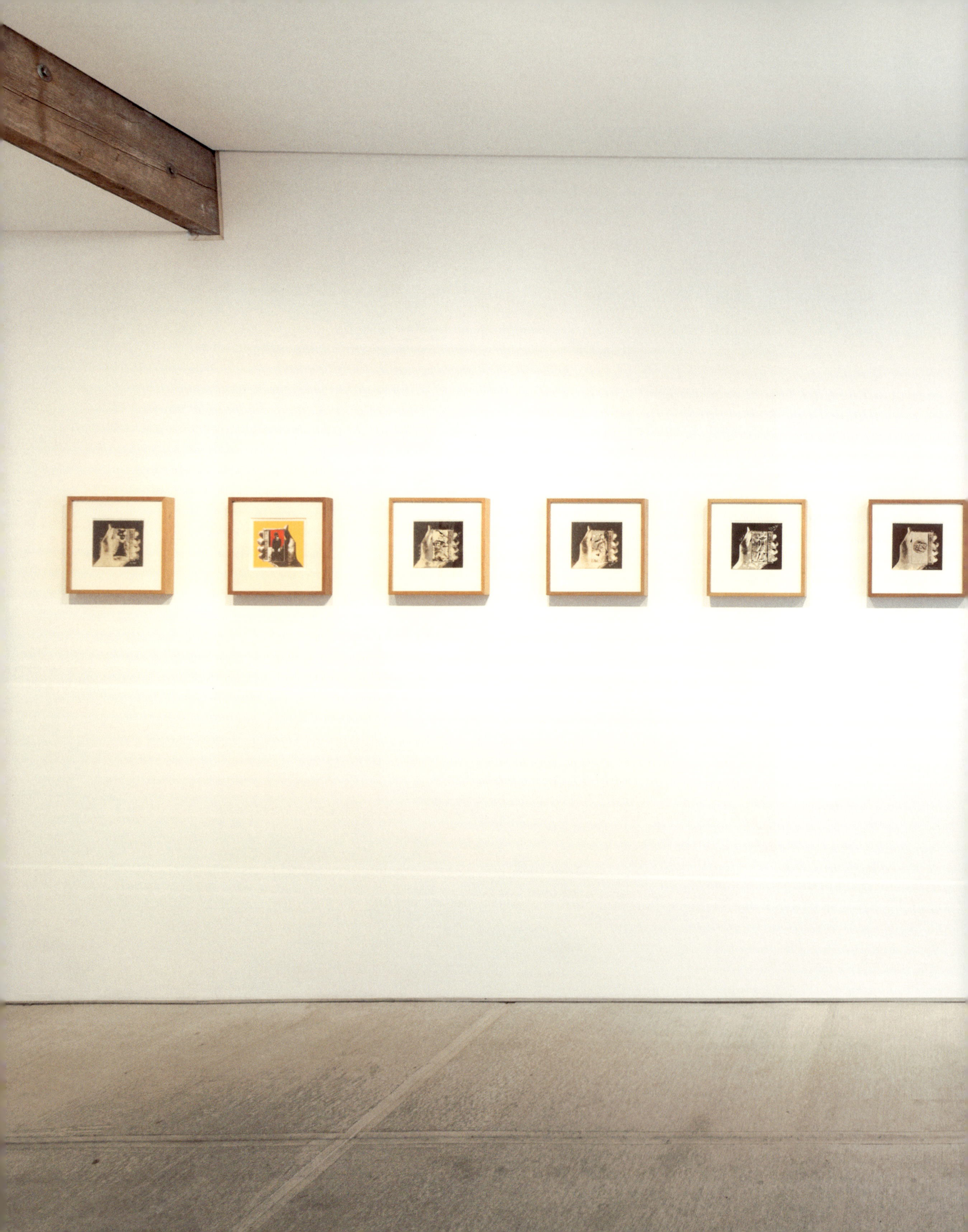

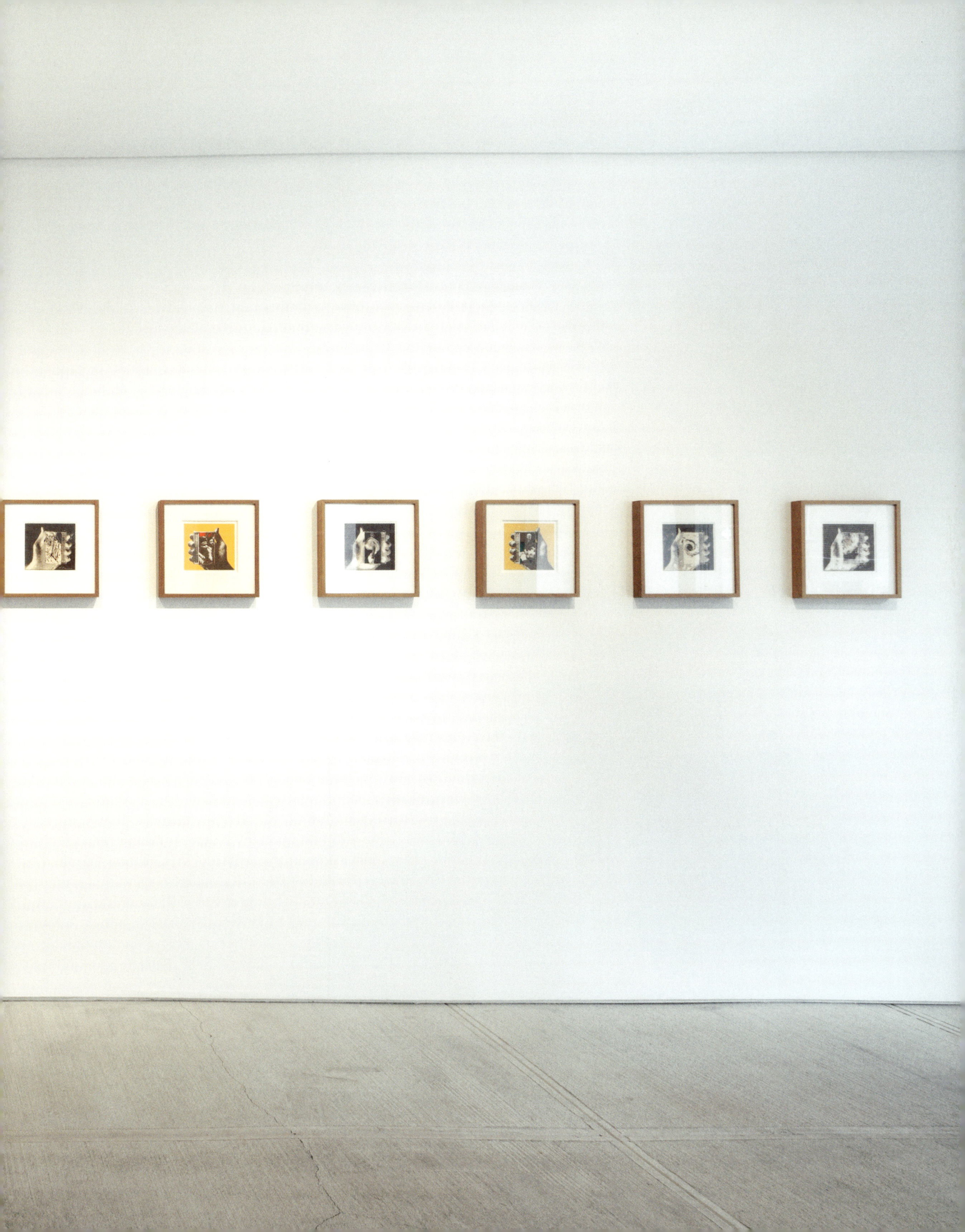

Untitled #7, c. 1964–76
single negative Verifax collage
6 × 6.5 inches (15 × 16.5 cm)

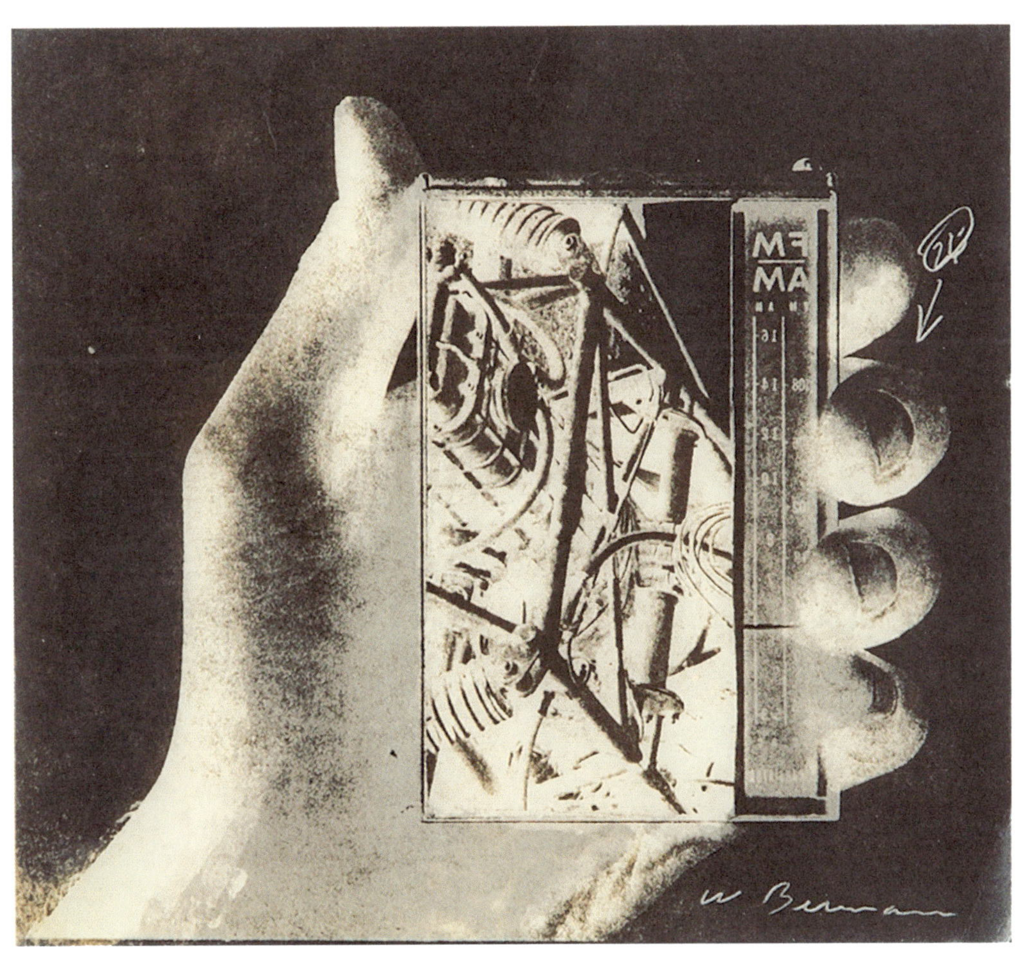
MF
MA
W Berman

Untitled #123, c. 1964–76
single Verifax collage with acrylic
6 × 6.5 inches (15.25 × 16.5 cm)

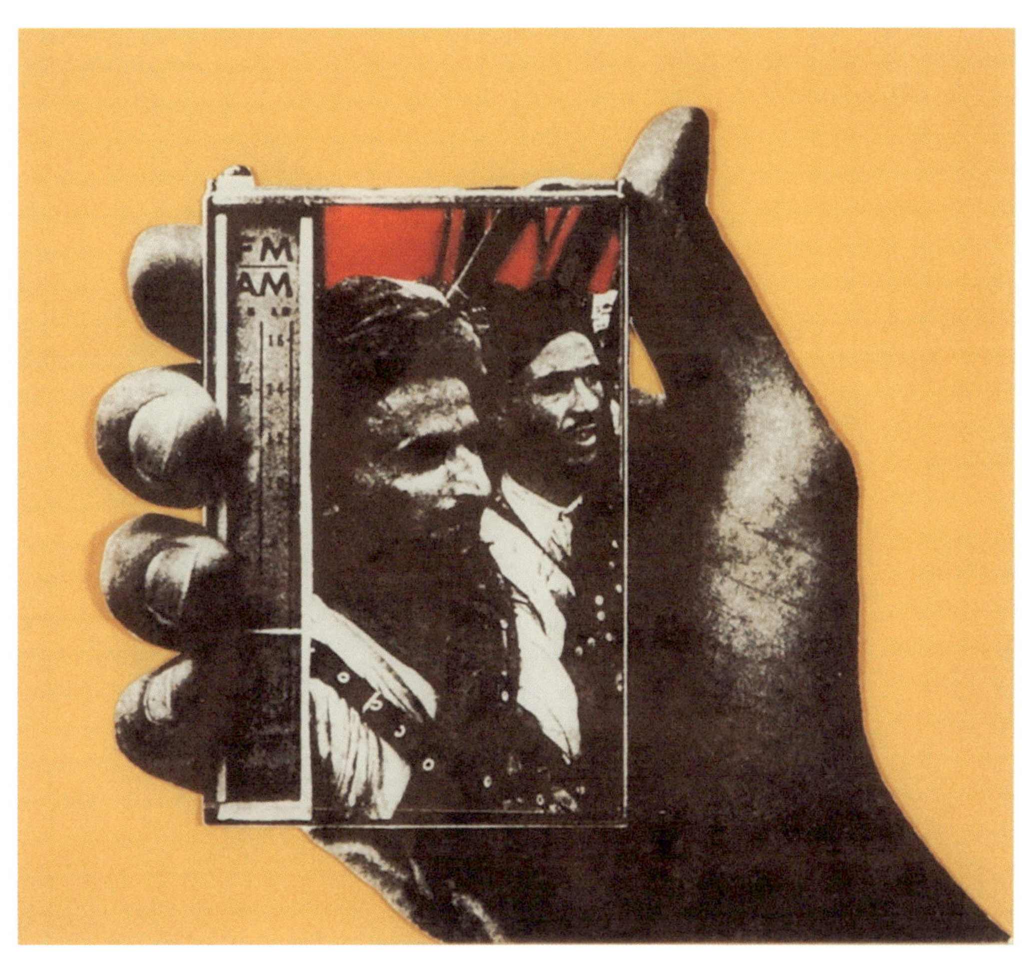
FM
AM

Untitled #86, c. 1964–76
single negative Verifax collage
6 × 6.5 inches (15 × 16.5 cm)

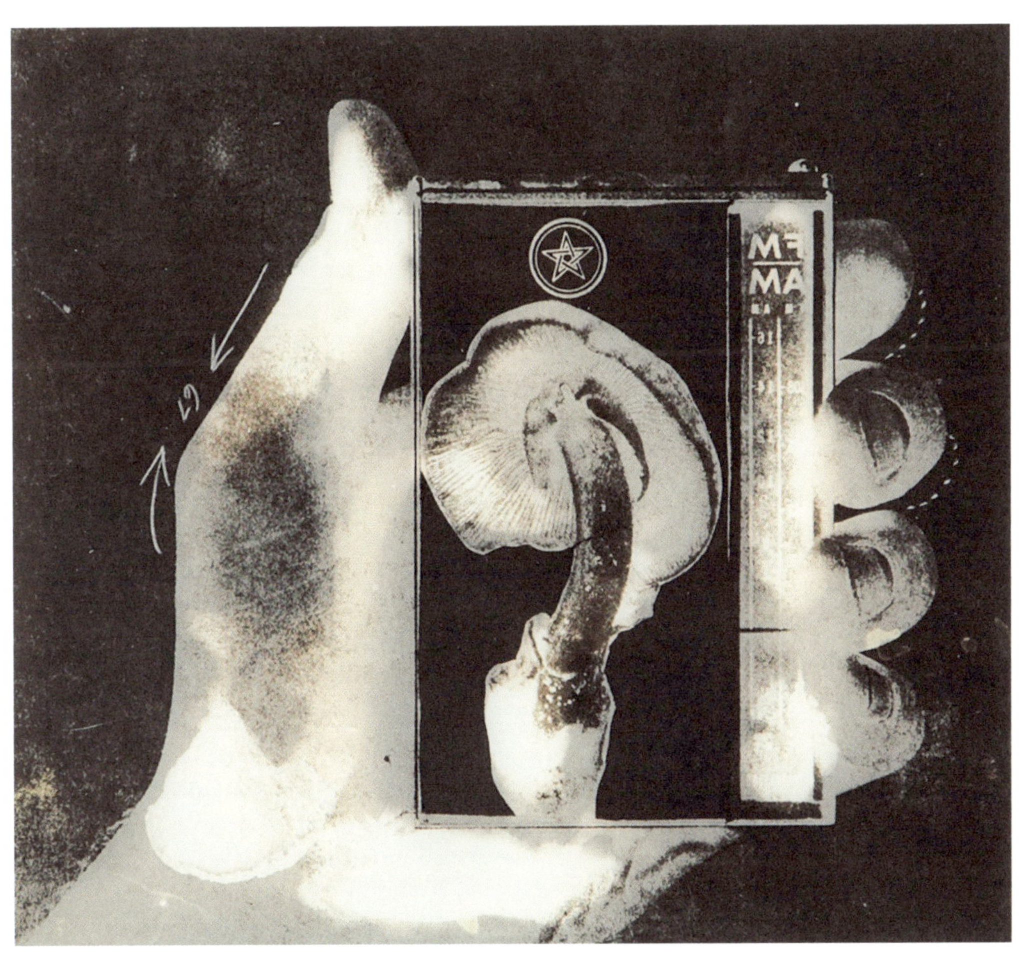

Untitled #119, c. 1964–76
single negative Verifax collage
6 × 6.5 inches (15 × 16.5 cm)

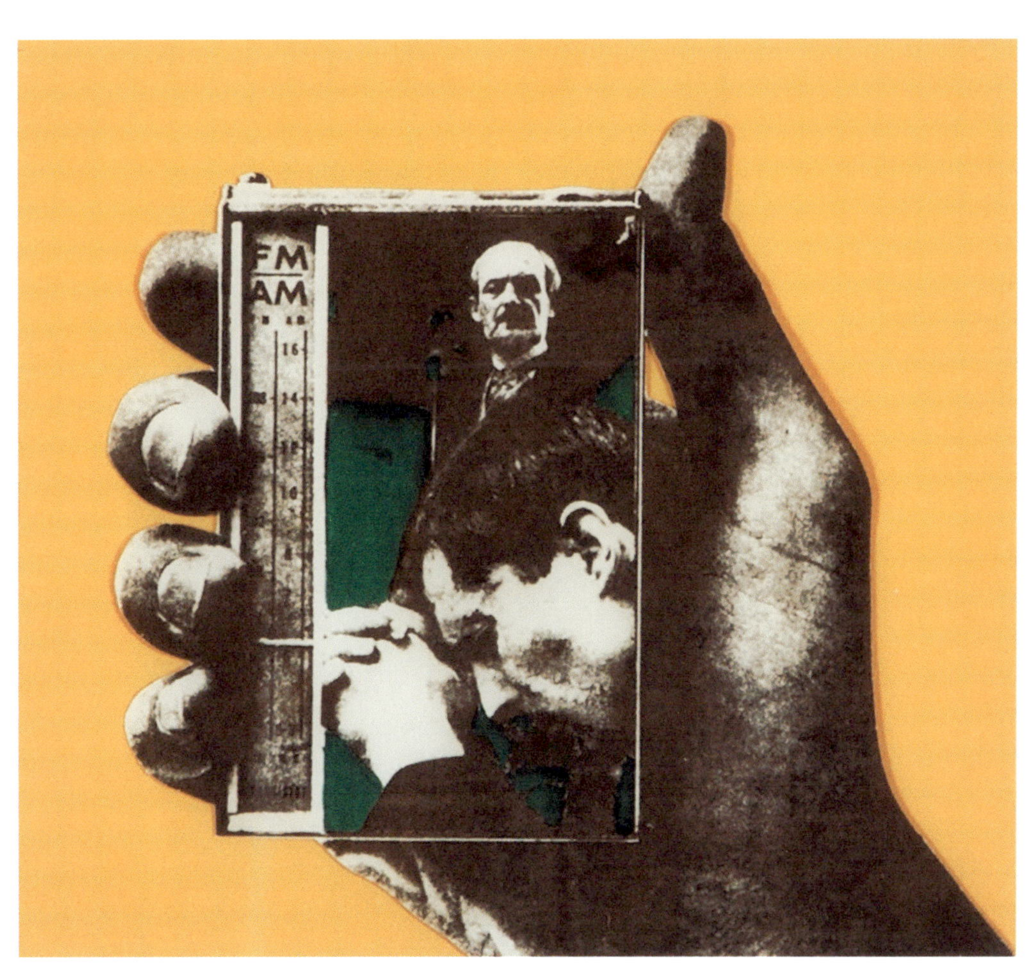
FM
AM

Untitled #79, c. 1964–76
single negative Verifax collage
6.5 × 6.5 inches (16.5 × 16.5 cm)

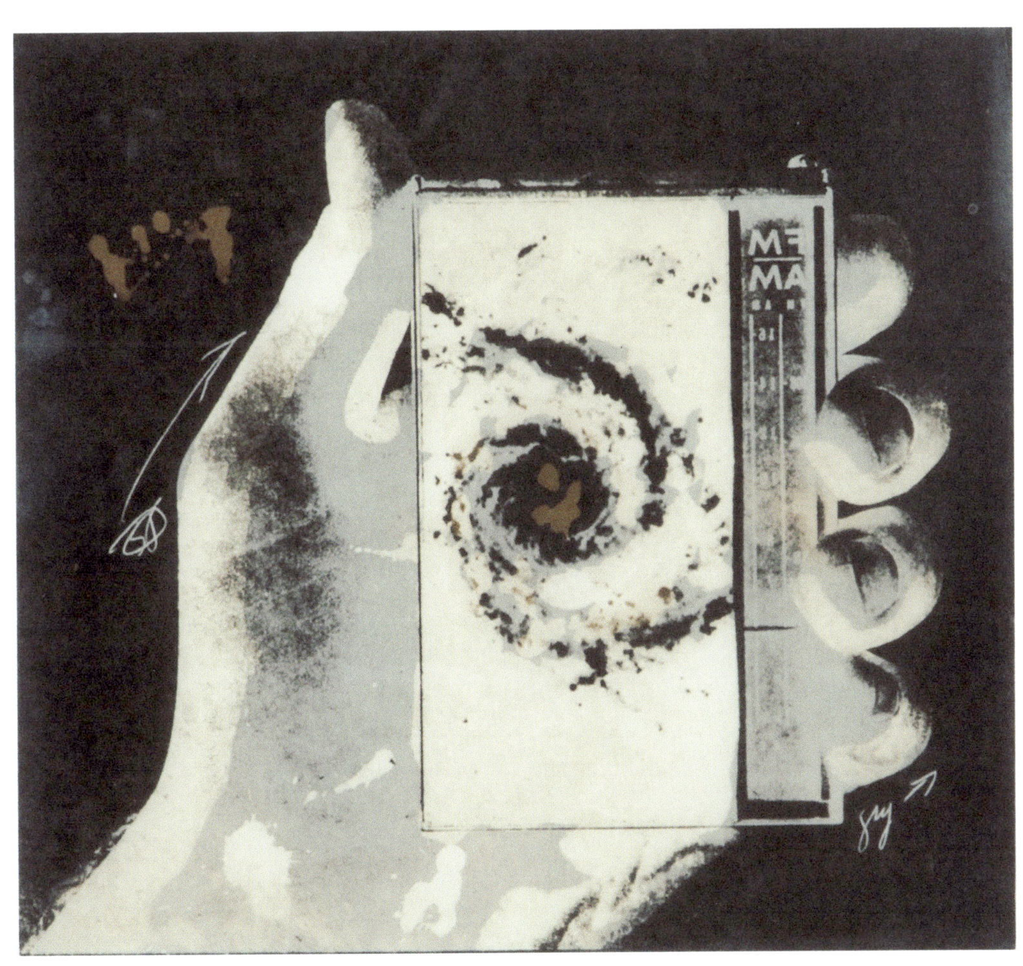

Untitled #40, c. 1964–76
single negative Verifax collage
6 × 6.5 inches (15 × 16.5 cm)

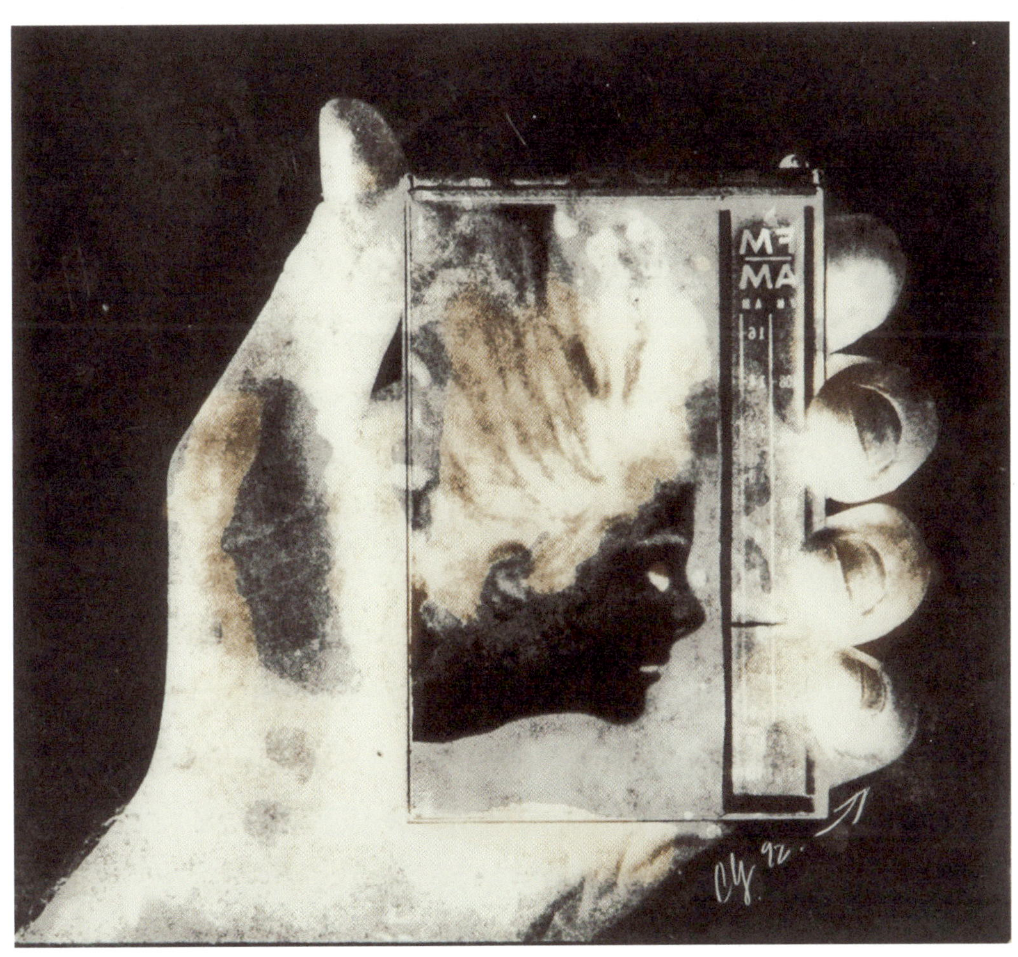

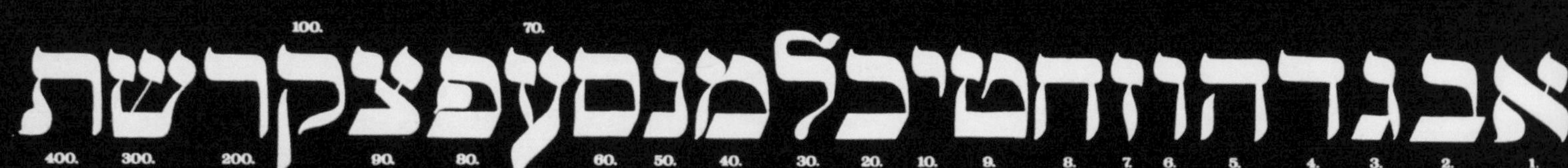

Radio Aether, 1966–1974
box of thirteen offset lithographs of the Verifax series
printed on Starwhite cover, mounted on Gemini Ragboard
12.25 × 14.25 inches (31 × 36 cm)
Edition 21 of 50

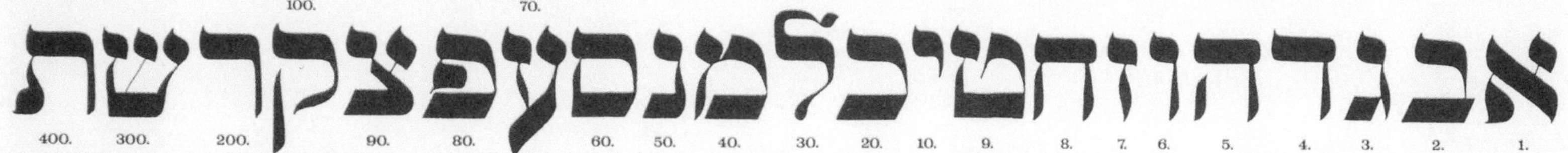

RADIO/AETHER SERIES 1966/1974

WALLACE BERMAN

13 OFFSET LITHOGRAPHS OF THE VERIFAX SERIES
PRINTED ON STARWHITE COVER MOUNTED ON GEMINI RAGBOARD
EDITION OF 50

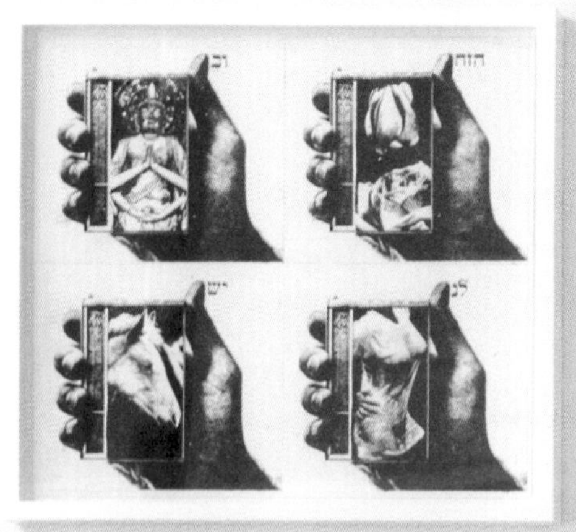
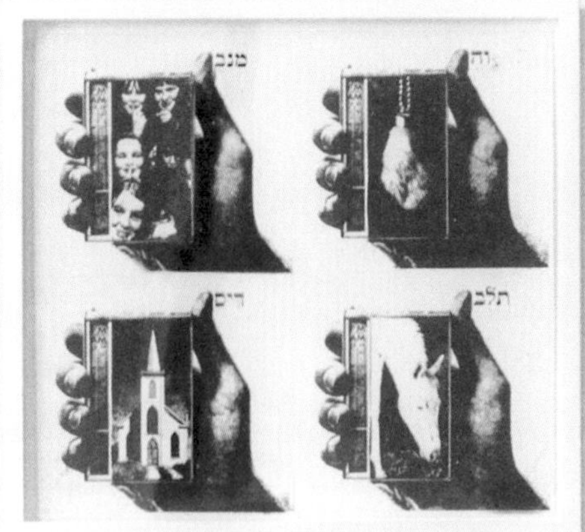
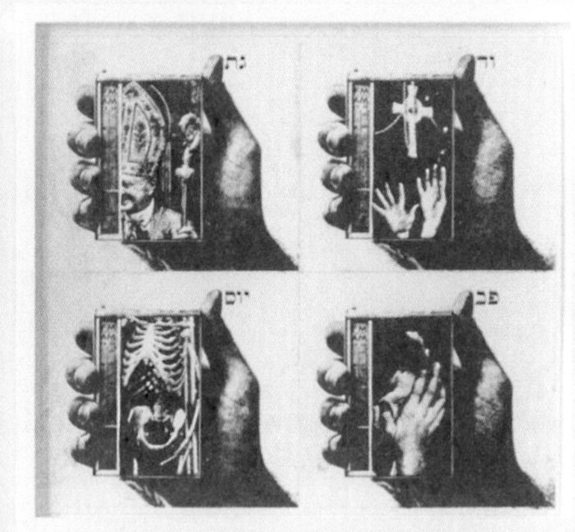
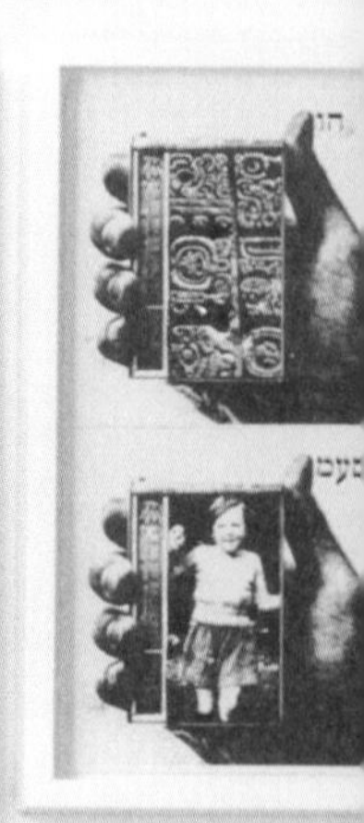
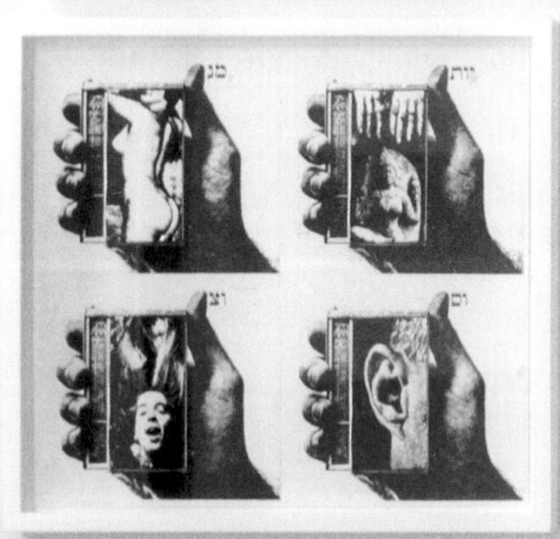
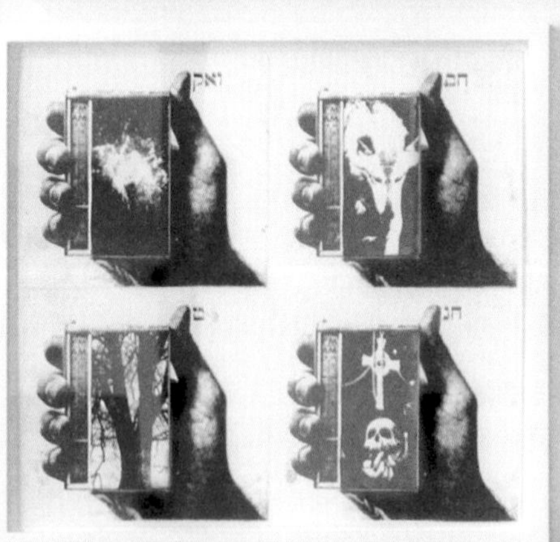
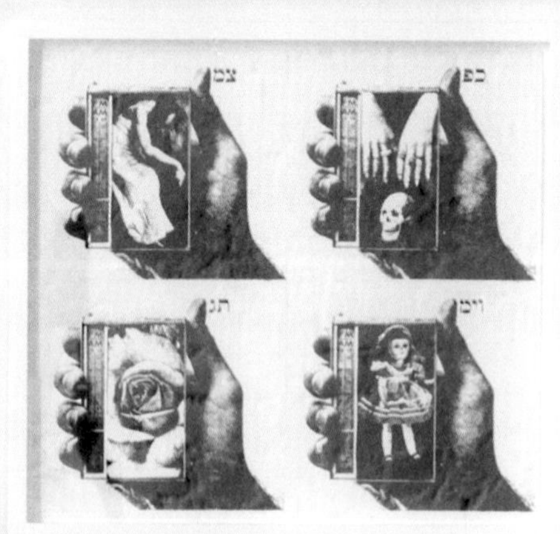
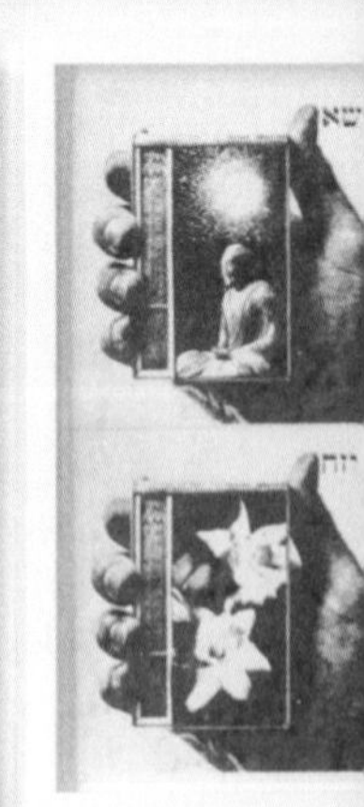

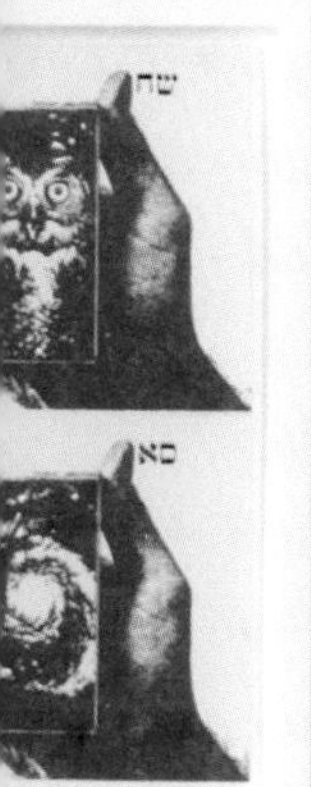
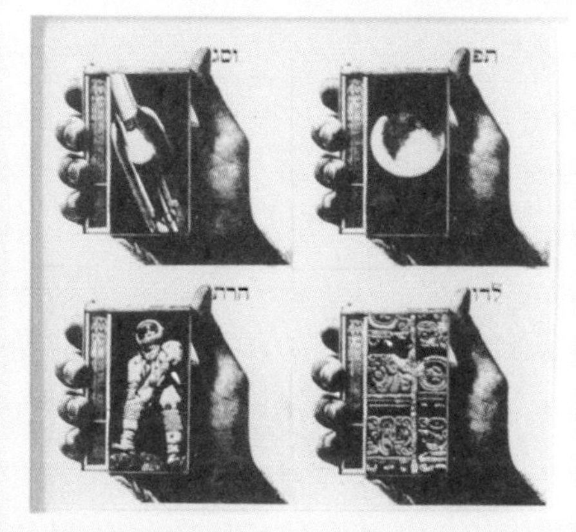
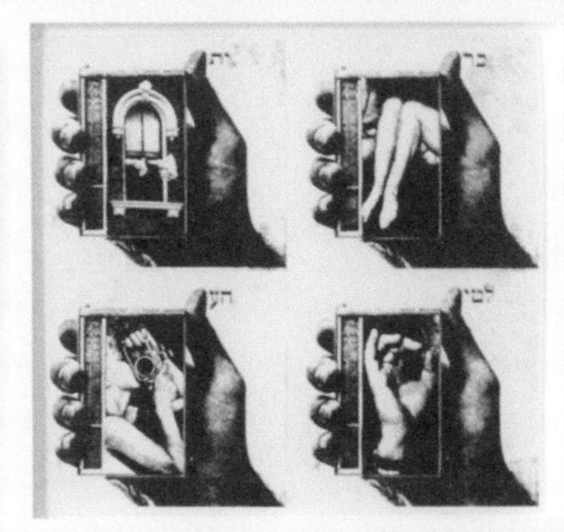
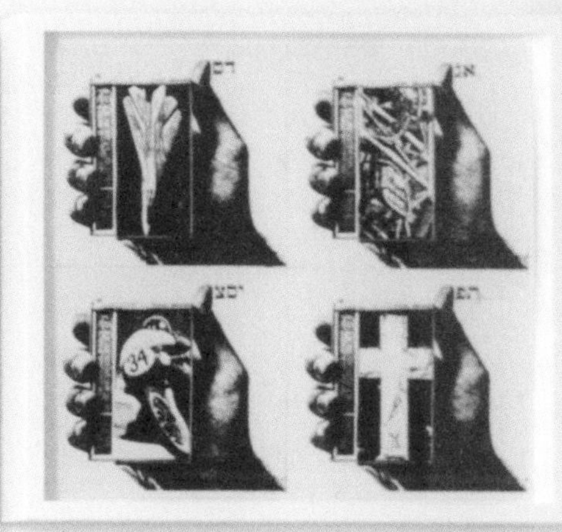
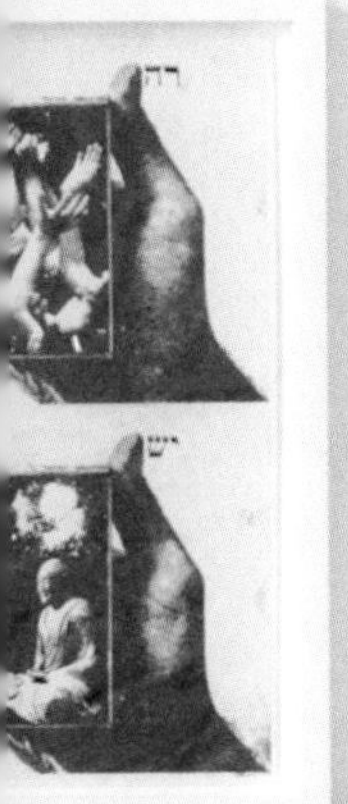
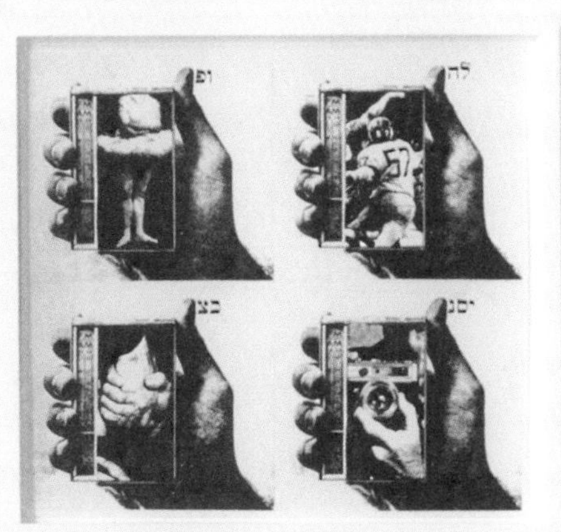
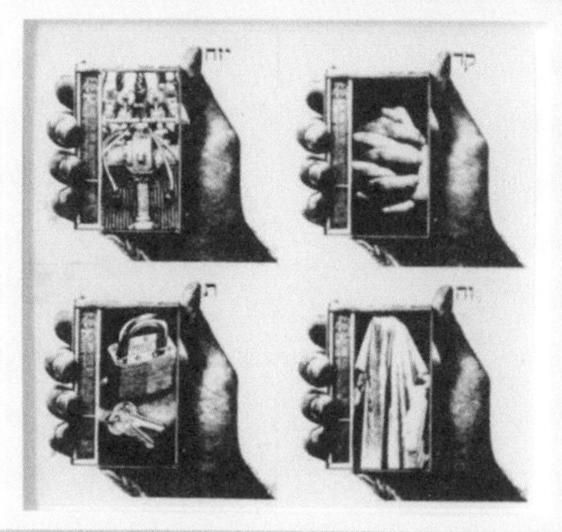

Untitled (Semina Gallery), 1961
modern inkjet print
20 × 16 inches (51 × 40.5 cm)

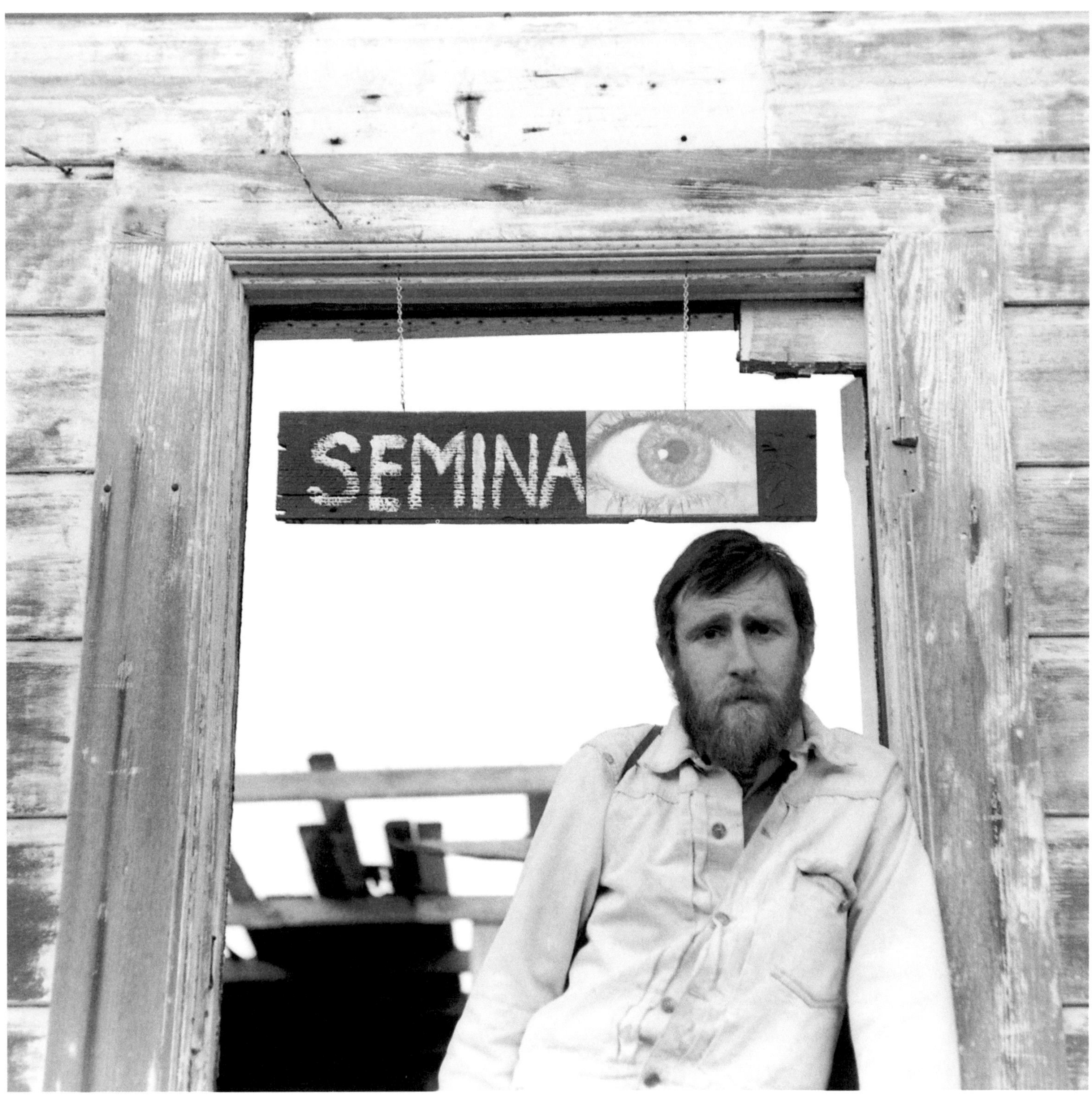
SEMINA

Untitled (Two-ton rock, two seals), c. 1964–76
polaroid transfer on magazine map
5 × 3.5 inches (13 × 9 cm)

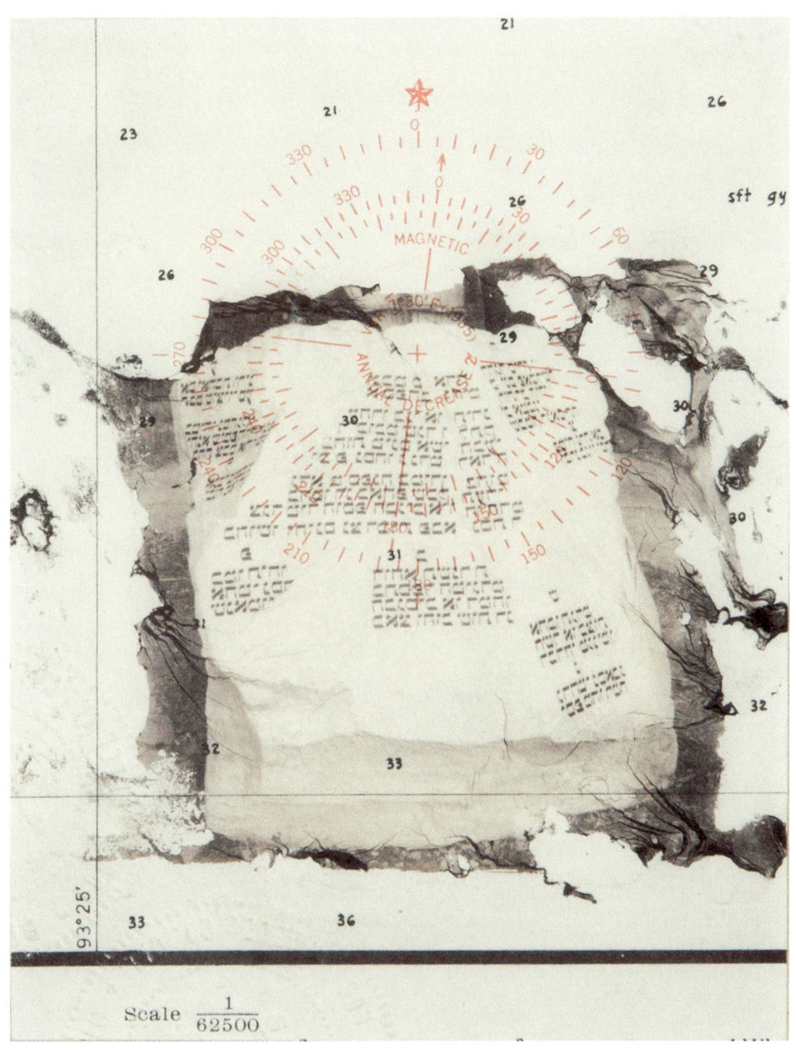
MAGNETIC
ANNUAL DECREASE
sft gy
93°25'
Scale 1/62500

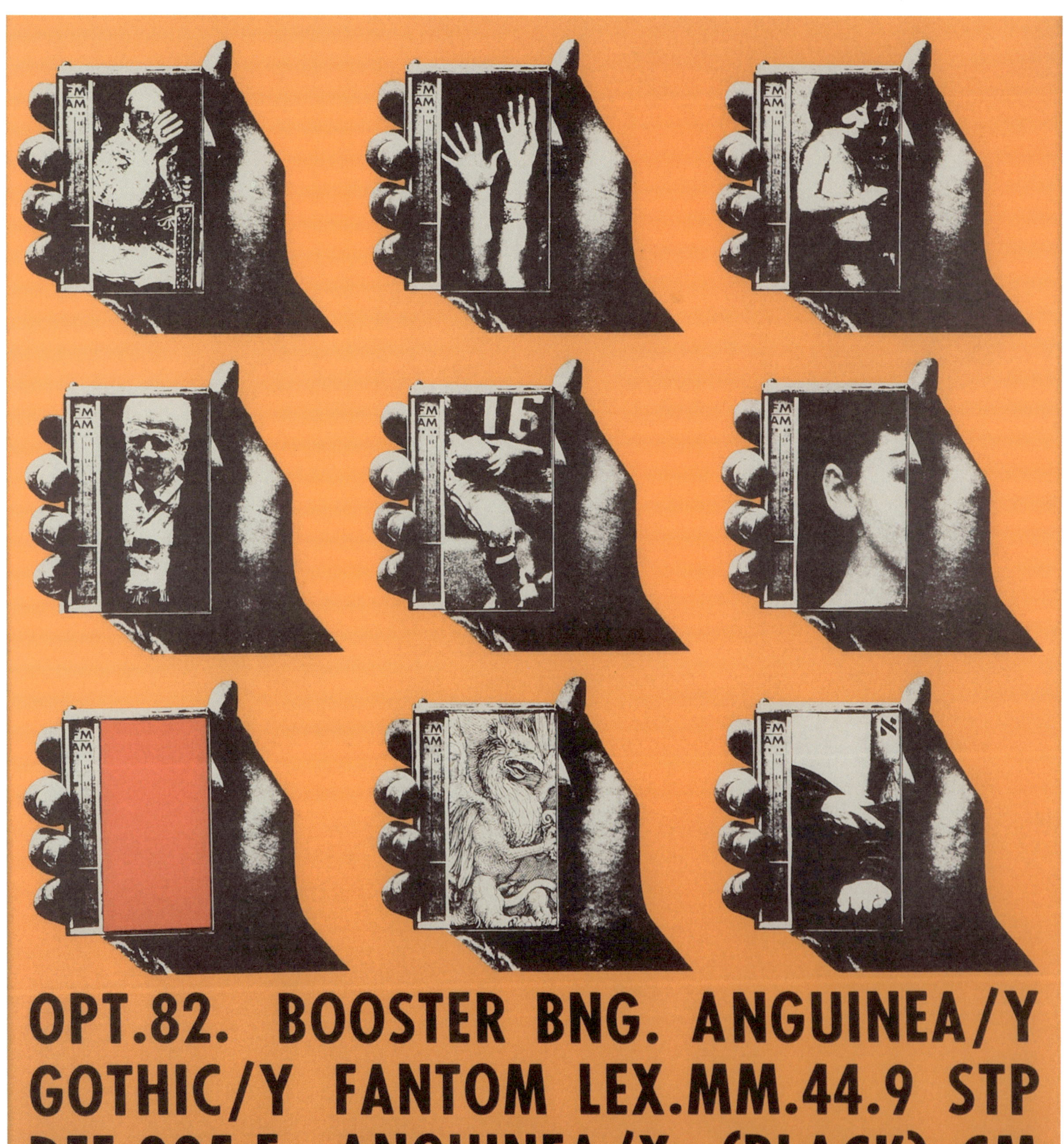

Untitled (Booster Bng), 1967
offset poster, published by John Martin
25 × 22 inches (63.50 × 56 cm)

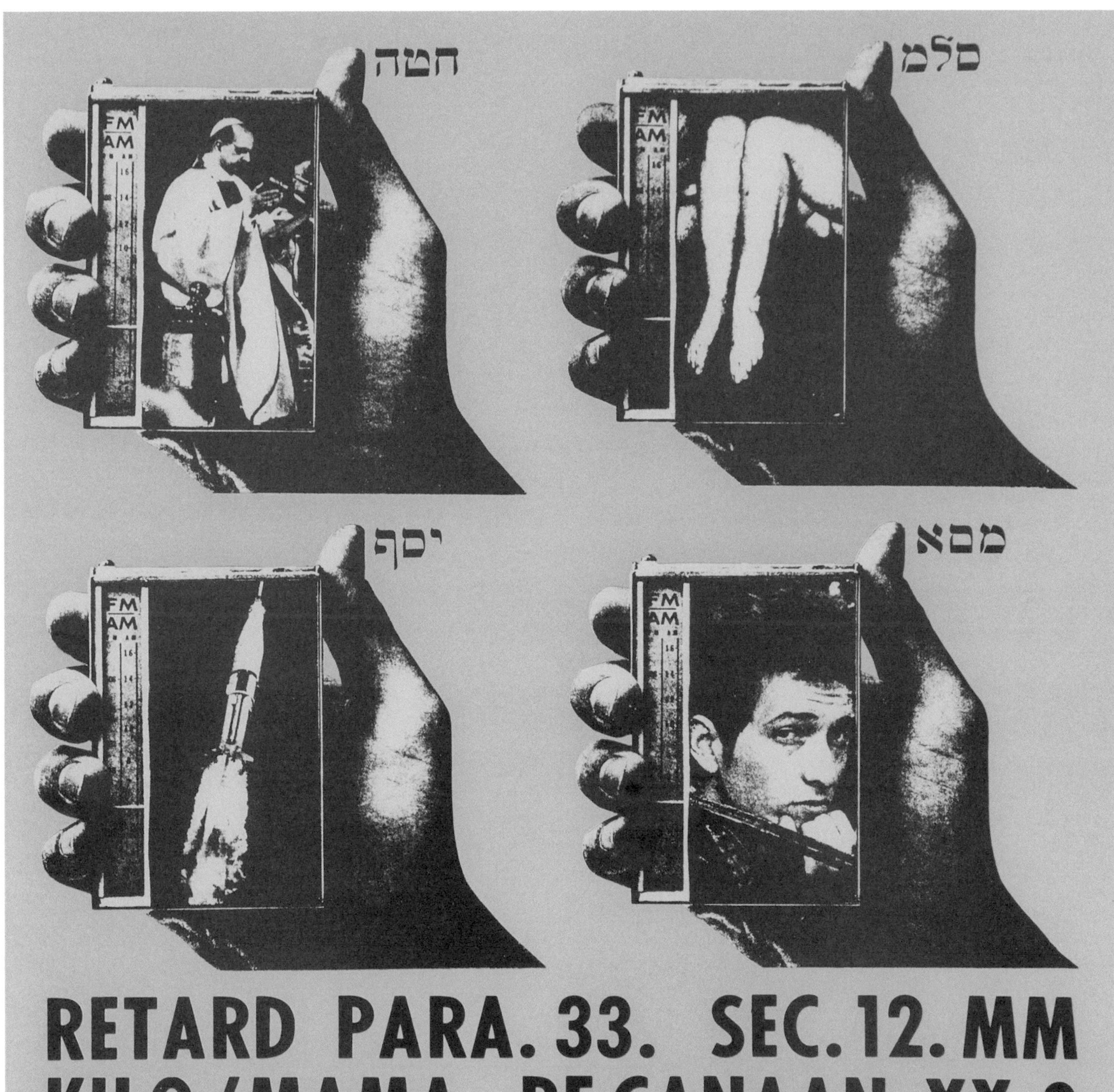

Untitled (Retard Para), 1965
offset poster
21 × 17 inches (53 × 43 cm)

Untitled (2nd Annual LA Filmmakers Festival), c. 1963
offset poster
20 × 16 inches (51 × 40.5 cm)

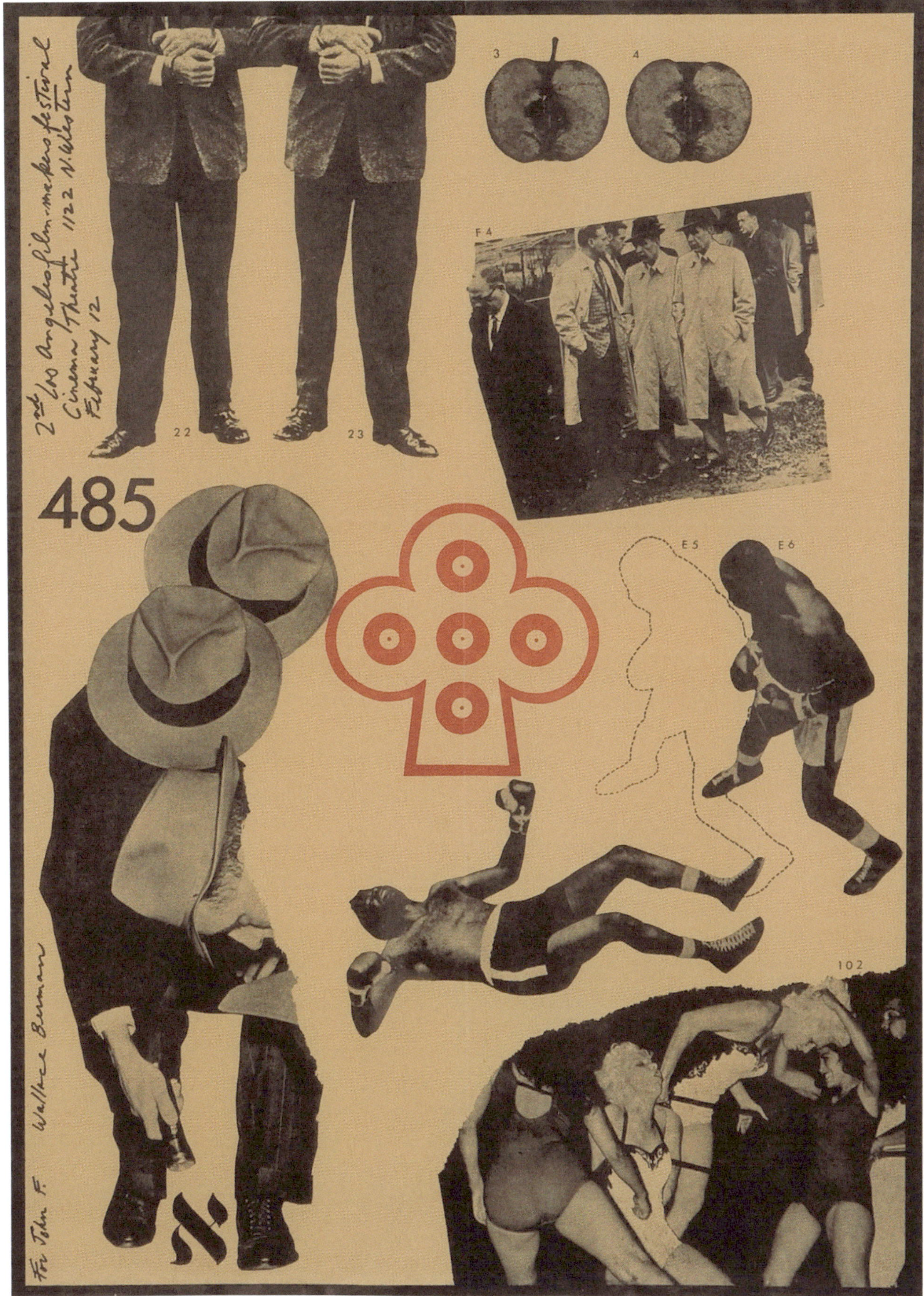
2nd Los Angeles film-makers festival
Cinema Theatre 1122 N. Western
February 12
3
4
22
23
F4
485
E5
E6
102
For John F. Wallace Berman
א

Wallace Berman: Re-Framed

by SAUL OSTROW

As vivid images of the horrors of the Holocaust and of mushroom clouds blossoming over Hiroshima and Nagasaki lingered in people's minds, a great migration west was begun in the post–World War II era. Unlike the Dust Bowl migration of the Great Depression, this one was a result of optimistic people seeking jobs associated with the mid-twentieth-century military-industrial complex and the new electronics industries. In popular culture, the promise of the good life that came with relocating to sunny California was celebrated in the sitcom TV series *The Life of Riley*, the storyline of which focused on the nuclear family of Chester A. Riley, a bungling wing riveter who has moved west to work at the (fictitious) Cunningham aircraft plant.

The antithesis of such wholesome father-know-best scenarios was the counterculture of the Beats and bebop jazz, which was taking root all along the West Coast, from Los Angeles to Seattle, and was popularized by mass media lifestyle coverage. By the early 1950s and '60s, an expansive community of freethinkers and political radicals expressing a desire to drop out and embrace nature and Eros had emerged. In L.A. this mindset nurtured a community of artists, poets, experimental theater companies, independent filmmakers, musicians, and others who, in their own ways, were aggressively antiestablishment.

Wallace Berman (1926–1976), whose family had moved from Staten Island, New York, to L.A. in the 1930s, was among the growing number of disenfranchised youths who believed "the war" had been fought to secure their individual freedom and rights. Emerging from the existentialist angst that gave birth to both the Beats and the Hells Angels (founded in 1947 in Fontana, California, fifty miles from L.A.), Berman set out to liberate himself. Denouncing materialism and conformity, he became a dissident—not from any particular social or political position but from the banality of the American Dream.

As with the Hells Angels, the romantic image of the outlaw—as an outsider, a free spirit bound to a nihilistic lifestyle—appealed to Berman. Rejecting the idea of conforming to the standards and values of the Establishment, Berman held the view that the continual production of the same monumental modernist culture that gave rise to the horrors of World War II would perpetuate a process fundamentally committed to commodifying and stifling freedom and creativity. This position was not out of pessimism, but a belief that he was promoting an extravagant vision of freedom and expression.

By the end of the fifties, Berman and his like-minded circle of friends and associates had established an outpost of vanguard culture on America's western frontier, making Berman one of the most important and influential artists to come out of the Los Angeles art scene of the fifties and sixties. This may seem like an outrageous statement given that, when we think of West Coast art of that era, the names that come more immediately to mind are Richard Diebenkorn, Sam Francis, Wayne Thiebaud, Ed Ruscha, John McCracken, James Turrell, and, maybe, Judy Chicago. Yet, unlike Berman, those artists fit the dominant account of American art, built on the triumph of Abstract Expressionism (the New York School), that portrays the West Coast assemblage and collage artists as out of sync with the trajectory of mainstream postwar culture.

Anything but provincial, Berman's milieu consisted of artists such as George Herms, Bruce Conner, Jess, Edward Kienholz, and Kenneth Anger, the actor/artist Dean Stockwell, the actor/director/photographer Dennis Hopper (who collected Berman's work), and an array of poets and musicians. He was also friends with the influential curator Walter Hopps, who gave Berman his first show, in 1957 at the seminal Ferus Gallery. When Hopps left to become the director of the Pasadena Art Museum, Irving Blum became the gallery's director. Today Ferus is best remembered because, in 1962, Blum organized the first show of Andy Warhol's *Campbell's Soup Cans* paintings. Given Berman's growing reputation,* in 1968 the young curator Kynaston McShine organized an exhibition of Berman's Verifax collages at the Jewish Museum in New York; at the time, the museum was known for showing cutting-edge contemporary art, having given Jasper Johns, Dan Flavin, Robert Rauschenberg, and Yves Klein their first museum shows, as well as organized such pioneering exhibitions as *Toward a New Abstraction*, *Primary Structures: Younger American and British Sculptors*, and the *Software* show.

On his fiftieth birthday, in 1976, Berman died in a car accident. In 1978, the Whitney Museum of American Art mounted a posthumous survey of Berman's Verifax collages; that same year, the Otis Art Institute, Los Angeles, organized *Wallace Berman Retrospective*. Then Berman slowly resided into the margins. The longer explanation as to what happened is that, while in time he would be proven to have been on the right side of history, he was on the wrong side of the critical debates taking place in the art world of the 1970s. At a time of momentous sociopolitical conflict, accompanied by a bacchanalia of sex, drugs, and disco, Berman's work, along with that of other artists of his generation who celebrated the abject, crude, and battered, had no place in an art world in which formalist abstraction was heralded: pop art celebrated consumer goods, comic books, and glossy advertisements, and the neoconstructivist machine aesthetics of minimalism were being canonized. By the 1970s, the counterculture of the 1950s was getting short shrift, and Berman and artists of his ilk were pushed aside and marginalized.

In December 1964, much of Berman's early photographs and negatives, sculptures, and drawings were destroyed when his house was demolished by a landslide. Though he continued to produce a diverse body of work, consisting of objects, collage paintings, photographs, posters, and the film *Aleph*, his best-known works are the collages he made using a Verifax machine (an early Kodak office photocopying machine) and *Semina*, a hand-printed folio of images and texts, by different artists and writers, that Berman produced,

---

* Berman's portrait appears directly above John Lennon's, two rows up, in the British pop artist Peter Blake's album cover for the Beatles' 1967 *Sgt. Pepper's Lonely Hearts Club Band*.

between 1955 and 1964, in limited numbers and distributed among his friends and contributors. The present exhibition, *Off the Grid*, consisting of forty-five works, demonstrates how Berman, by substituting a range of appropriated imagery, was able to generate a wide variety of contextual and associative interpretations.

Like Rauschenberg's assemblages (which he branded "combines") and Allan Kaprow's collage paintings of photographs, texts, objects, and mirror fragments, Berman's work sits on the cusp of pop art. Yet, rather than blowing up and monumentalizing the vacuousness of popular culture, Berman's pop is at once transient and intimate, conveying a sense of mystery and awe. In his work he juxtaposed imagery of machines, bodies, animals, buildings, plants, nuns, athletes, astronauts, guns, nebulae, rock stars, and celebrities, along with references to current events, Hebrew letters and Kabbalistic signs (perhaps as reminders of the Holocaust), and a wide range of poetic allusions. Starting with an image of a portable TV taken from an advertisement, Berman would eventually settle on a hand holding a portable AM/FM transistor radio; where the radio's speaker should be, he collaged his encyclopedic universe of imagery.

When adapting his work to the Verifax, a means of mechanical reproduction, Berman abandoned his torn-and-scattered aesthetic, instead gathering the various Verifax collages into grids that ranged from four to fifty-six images. The grid, which Berman began using in 1963, with four TV collages, permits the viewer to see each image as an icon while at the same time being inundated with potentially endless associations and interpretations. Warhol, who had spent time with Berman in L.A., adopted a similar strategy, to different ends. Warhol's grids of movie stars, Coke bottles, et cetera, emphasized the sameness and repetition of his images, while Berman's images generated associative narratives. Berman's use of the grid most likely stemmed from his interest in comics, trading cards, and the tarot rather than geometric abstract art and supermarket shelves, Warhol's probable source.

Though they draw on differing traditions—Warhol informed by the master narratives of Abstract Expressionism and formalist abstraction, Berman rooted in the heritage of Symbolism and Dadaism—it is reasonable to compare them, given that both were responding to similar mainstream cultural and social stimuli. To do so only formally (e.g., their use of the grid, repetition, mechanical reproduction, and ready-made imagery) is to fail to recognize the differences in their ambition and effect; Warhol used reproduction as a means to make the sociopolitical impersonal, while Berman strove for the inverse. Warhol used photographic silkscreens and a crew of studio assistants to mass-produce his repetitive-image "paintings," while Berman used his old Verifax office copier to appropriate symbols that had the potential to seduce, control, and corrupt.

To get to the inner workings of Berman's image stream, one has to tear away the bohemian romanticism and the eccentricities of biography.* Stripped bare of the anecdotal, what is revealed is Berman's commitment

---

* The story is that Berman was an attention-getting adolescent who dressed in zoot suits and an award-winning swing dancer who hung around the jazz clubs. He was also a hustler, making money by dealing pot or playing craps. Expelled from Fairfax High, discharged from the navy, and tossed out of Chouinard Art Institute, he set himself up as an artist in L.A. His show at Ferus Gallery in 1957 was shut down by the police for its inclusion of an erotic drawing. For this Berman went to jail. The trauma led him to move to San Francisco and then Larkspur, California, for a few years. Returning to L.A., he became the center of a legendary group of artists, musicians, and poets committed to the Beat ethos and personal freedom. Among other things, he opened a gallery and self-published *Semina*, a journal of poetry and images. He also seemingly knew or met everyone on the cutting edge of culture along the West Coast. If this were not spectacular enough, Berman died in a car crash on his fiftieth birthday.

to the use of art to sustain the trauma of the war period by abolishing the notion that art is an activity separate from life or a means of escape into a world of fantasy or indifference. An important part of Berman's project was to politicize aesthetics, "liberate the imagination," and alter consciousness. To do this, he and his compatriots incorporated absurdity, disorder, nonsense, disorientation, and the detritus of everyday life into an assault on an aloof and indifferent culture of refinement. With the acquisition of the Verifax machine, Berman could capture, reproduce, and manipulate the flotsam and jetsam of the visual data stream representing contemporary life. By adopting a vocabulary of ready-made images, a mechanical means of reproduction, and a conception of art as performative, Berman mediated between the personal and the pervasive commercialization and commodification of culture and its contingent evils, rather than cynically celebrating the culture of commodity fetishization and consumerism, as Warhol did.

Seen from an international perspective, Berman and his associates are not practioners of some minor movement or regional style that achieved local mythic status or a cultish aura. In their objectives they were aligned with other postwar groupings, including the Situationist International, British pop and the Independent Group, French nouveau réalisme, Italian arte povera, and the international network known as Fluxus, all of which are shown and referenced in the United States only minimally. These highly influential movements used elements taken from the fabric of everyday life to transform the cultural arena into a battlefield.

So, when Berman and his genres are overlooked or ignored, what is actually being denied is the international counterculture that stood in opposition to Cold War myths about the freedom and progressiveness of Western society's consumer culture. Because this critique has been neither duly appropriated nor abandoned, its message and aesthetic persist within today's subcultures. Correspondingly, *Off the Grid*, the largest exhibition of Berman's work in New York since the Whitney Museum show in 1978, demonstrates that Berman's vision remains prescient, offering up a model of what may still be done in the name of addressing the contingent evils of commercialization and commodification in this age of conformity.

ALEPH

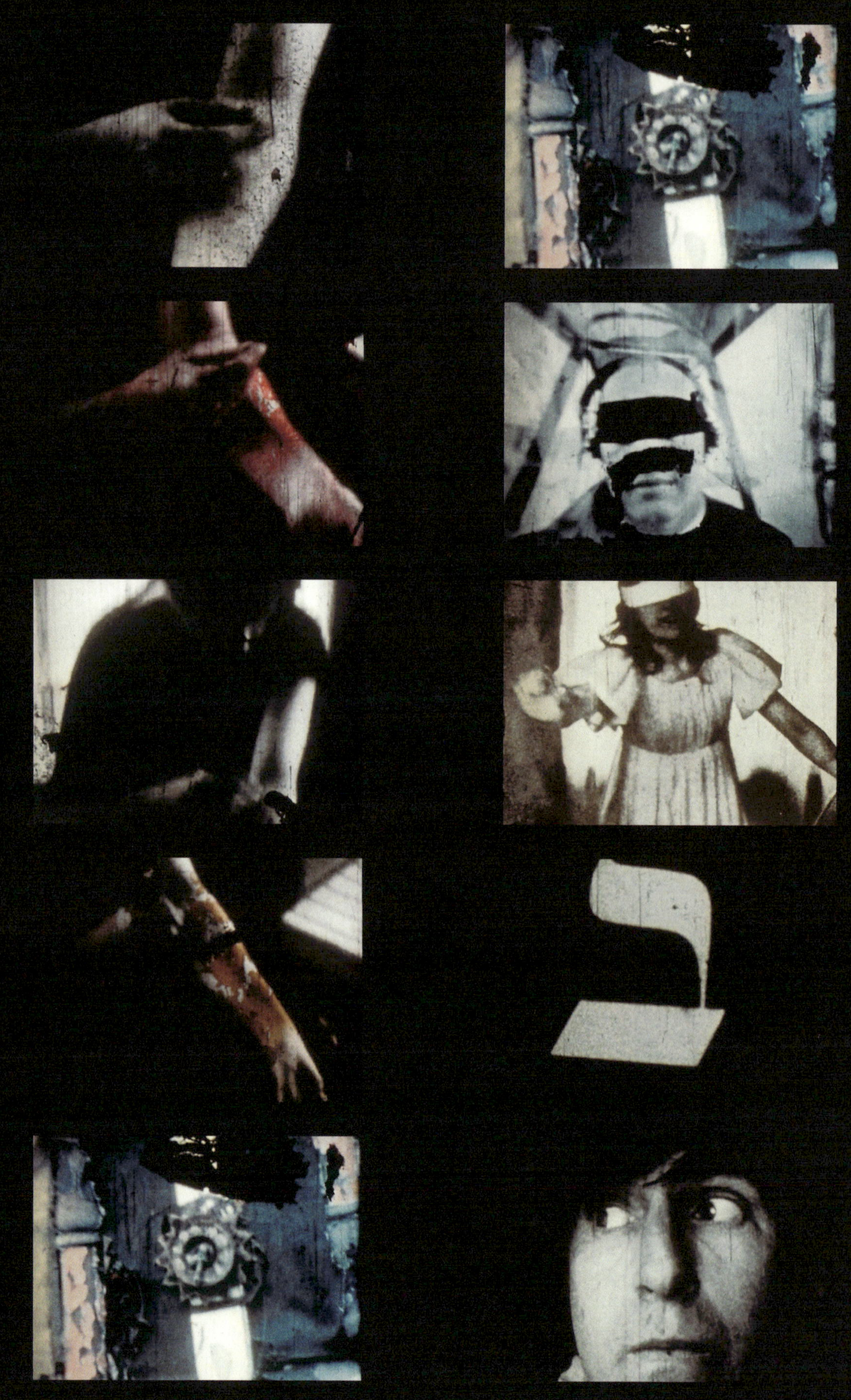
ב

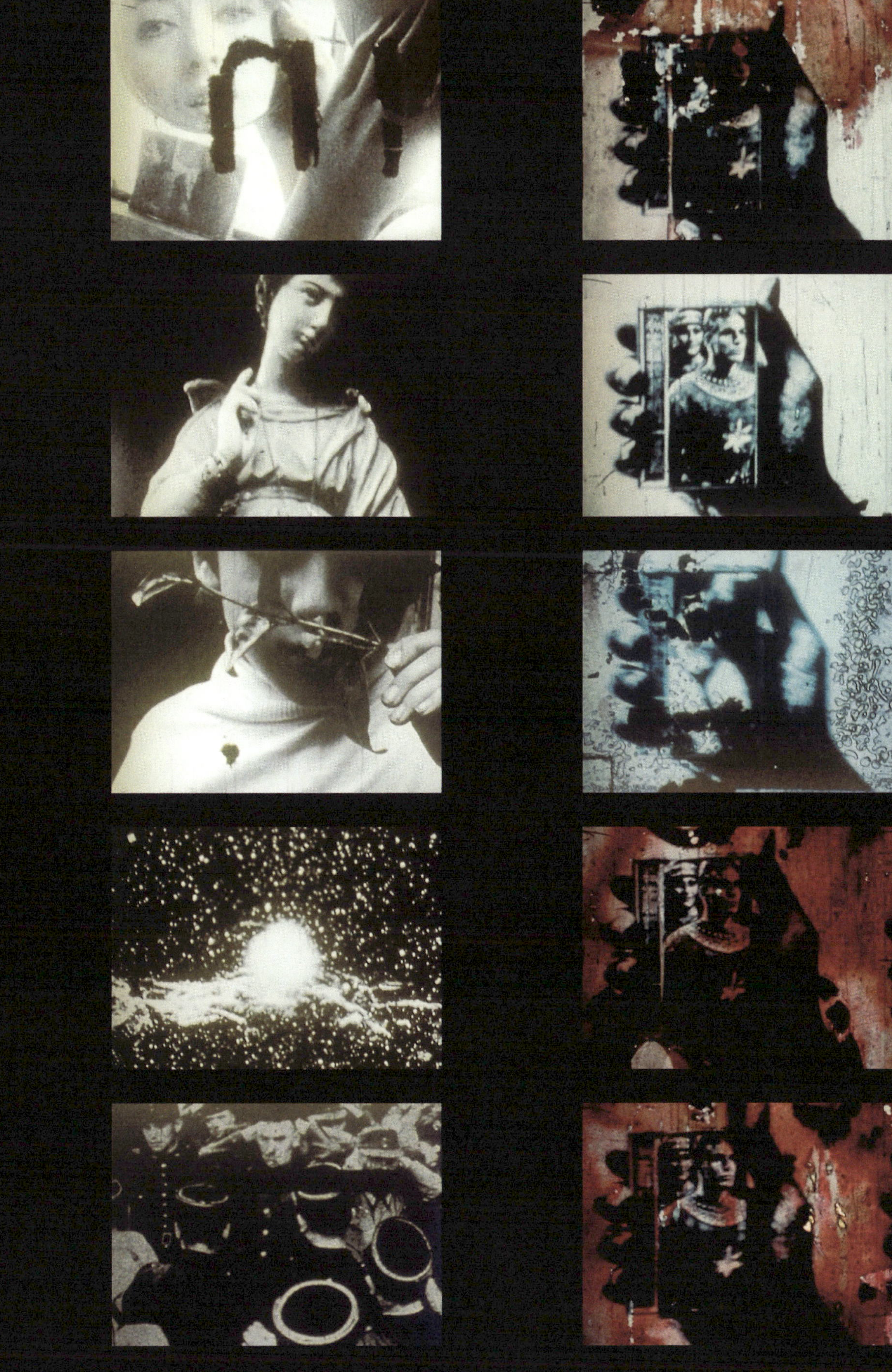

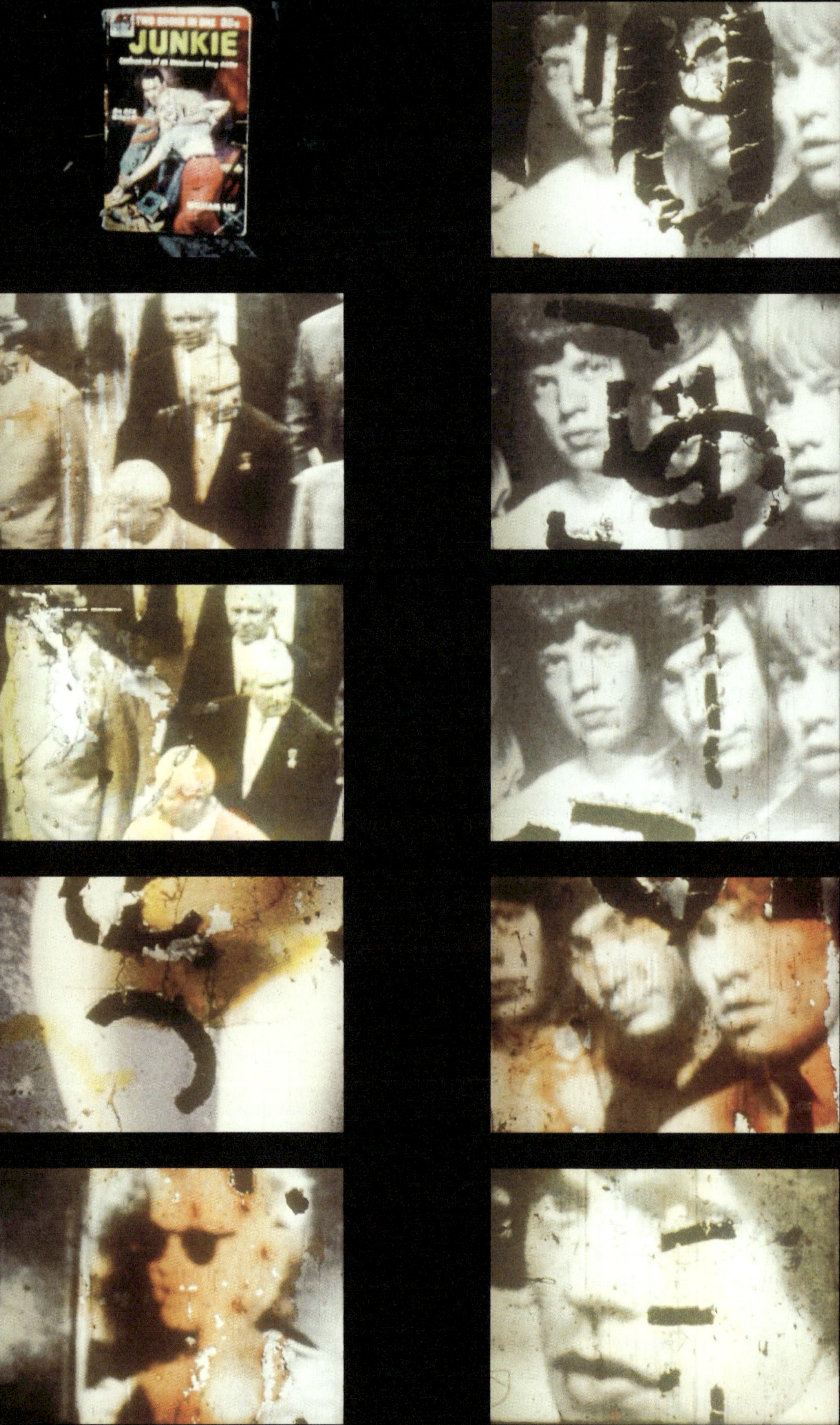
JUNKIE

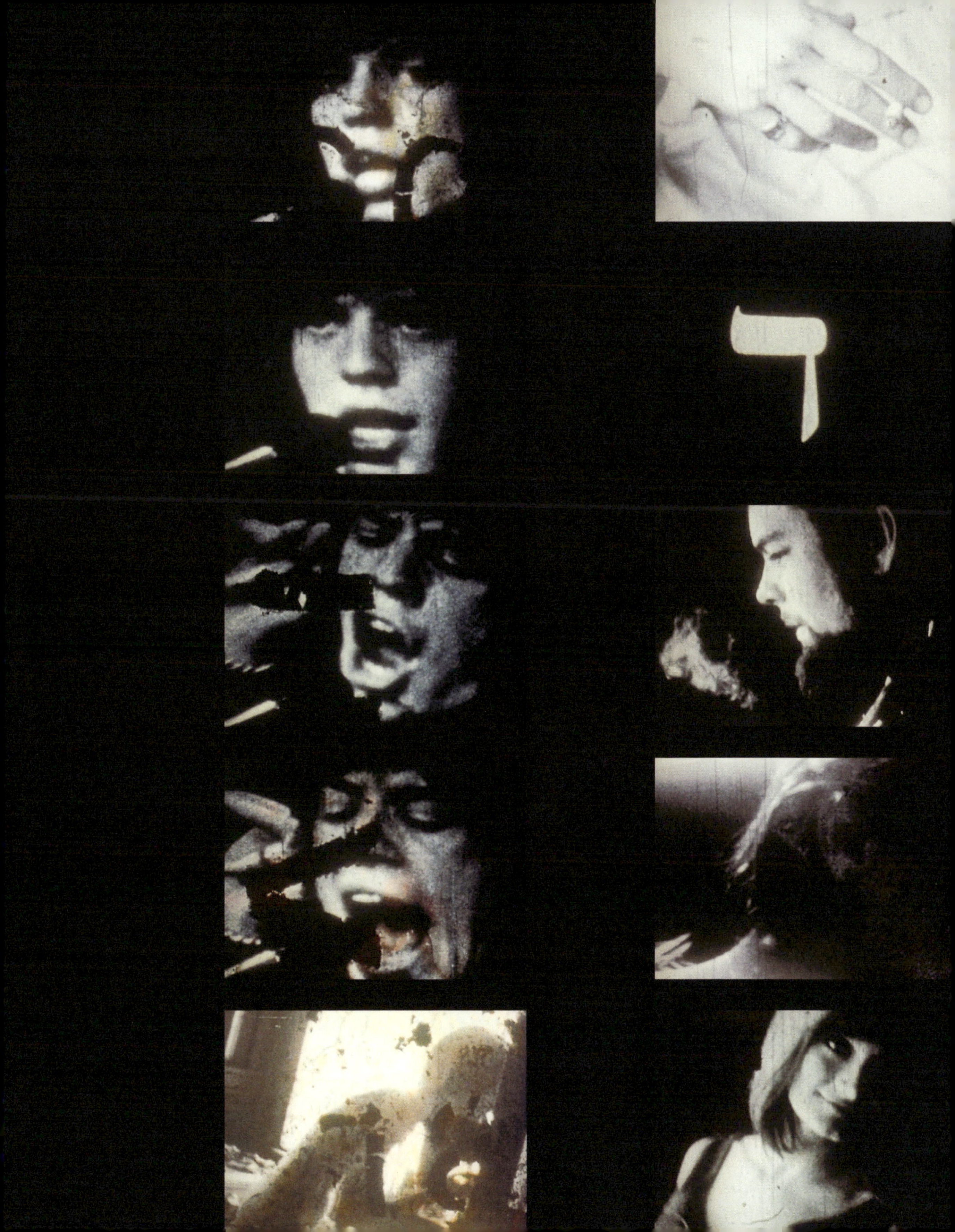
ק

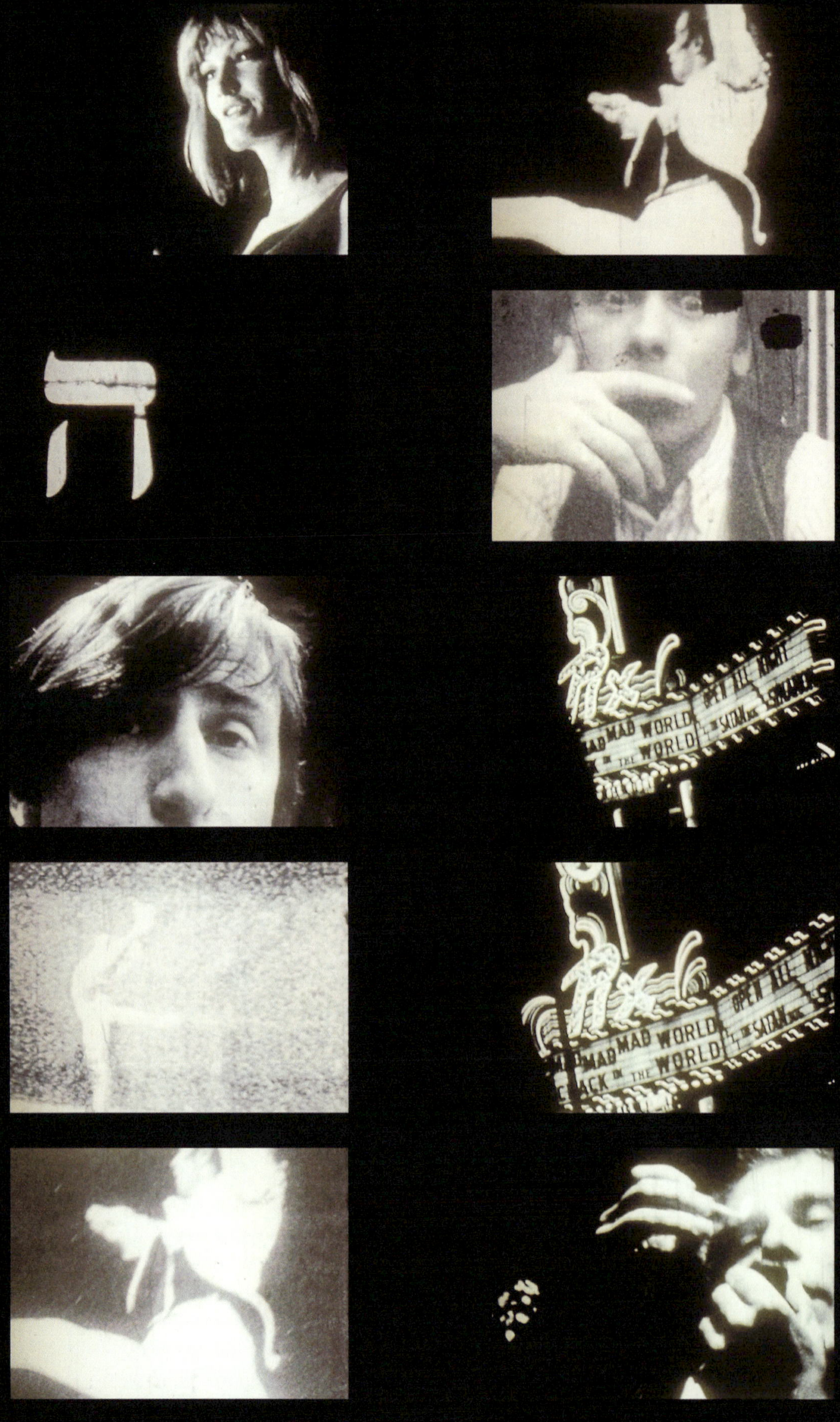
MAD WORLD
THE WORLD
OPEN ALL NIGHT
SATAN

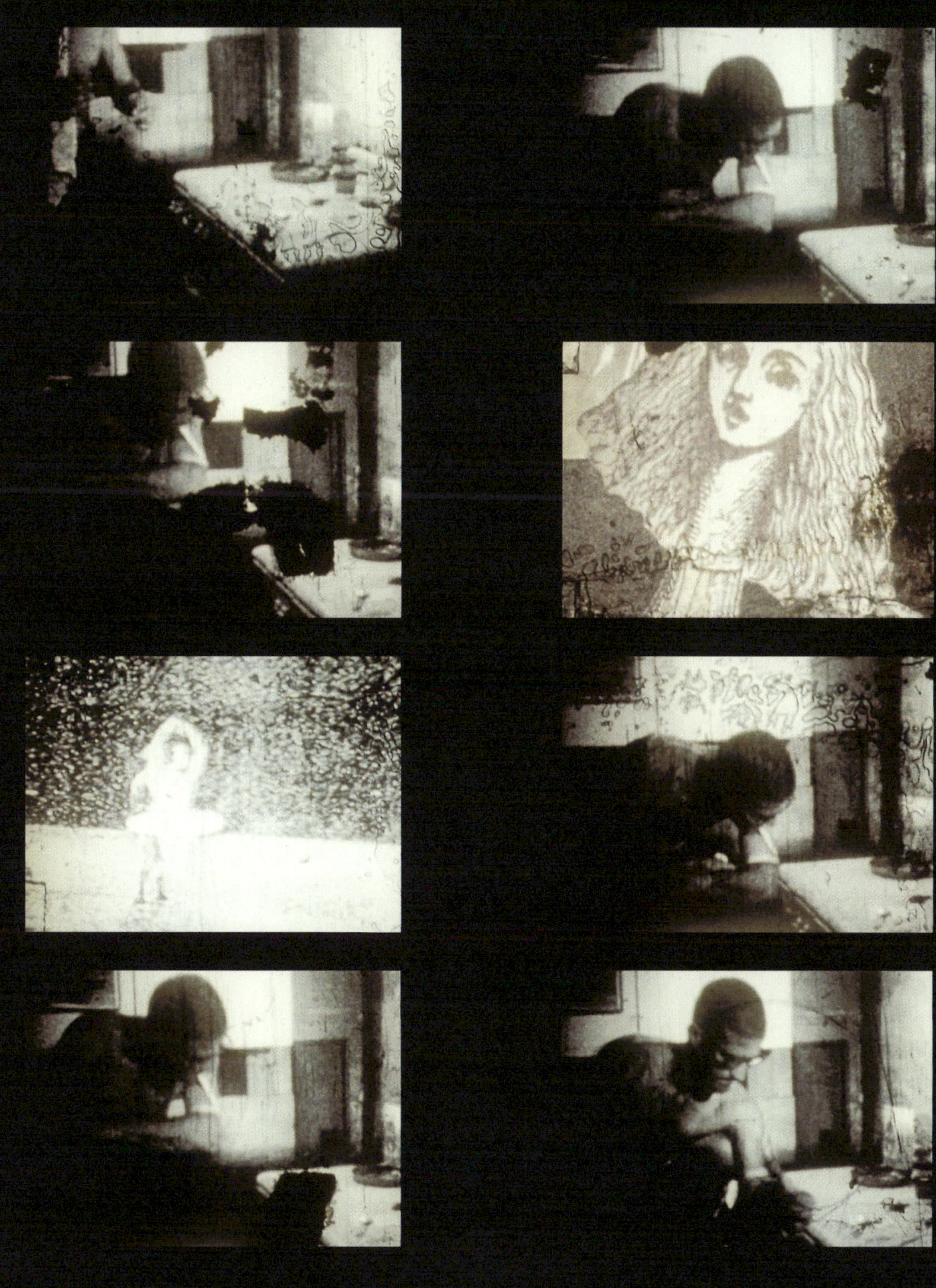

Wallace Berman
Aleph, 1956–66
16mm film transferred to video (black-and-white, silent)

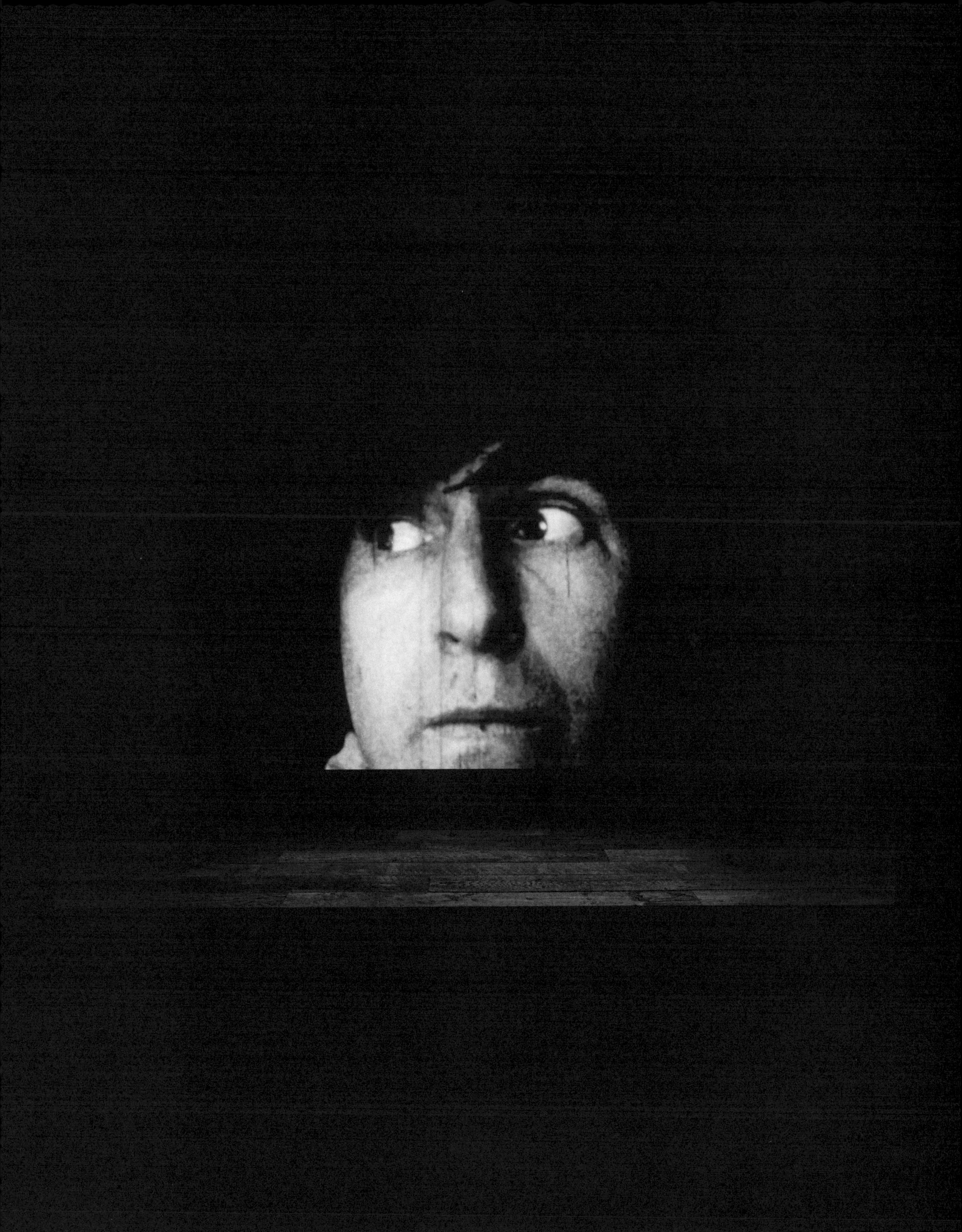

Tosh Berman and Andrew Lampert
discuss Wallace Berman's film

ALEPH

Moderated by Anne Waldman
September 18, 2021, at TOTAH, New York

Anne Waldman

Here we are on the day of the memorial to the insurrection in DC, when its defendants gather near the Capitol grounds to protest justice for their antithesis reality—the antithesis of *Aleph;* we can talk more about that later. First some quick bios. Tosh is such a genius, and has come all this way to be here, in the legacy, in the archive, in his glory, and in the light. Some of you probably know all, or some of his work. He's written three titles: *Tosh: Growing Up in Wallace Berman's World*, *Sparks-Tastic: Twenty-One Nights with Sparks in London*, and a book of poems, *The Plum in Mr. Blum's Pudding.*

We have Andrew Lampert, who's a major figure in the culture of this town and beyond. A filmmaker himself, who worked for years at Anthology Film Archives, with Jonas Mekas, he is an incredible lineage holder and also an active artist, as both these gentlemen are. He cofounded the firm Chen & Lampert, his work has been internationally exhibited in venues including the Whitney, the New York Film Festival, the Getty Museum, and the Toronto Film Festival, and he's edited books on Tony Conrad, Harry Smith, Manuel DeLanda, and George Kuchar.

This film, *Aleph*, is about time—the very short lines of time, the attention to the minute energies and icons within each syllable, so that each syllable becomes a kind of power. How are you holding time? How are you holding image? How are you holding voice? How are you holding gesture in a kind of liminal space that keeps waking the world up to itself?

I'm going to let them both take it forward from here, from inside *Aleph*.

Tosh Berman

My father started making this film, *Aleph*, in the 1950s, and I think it ended when he died, in the sense that he may still have worked on it even to this day if he were alive. But to me it does have a beginning and an end. The beginning is Bob Alexander, a close friend of my father and a fellow artist of that time, about to shoot up, and then the end of the film is him actually doing it. I always felt that was the framework of what he was working on—it was not a narrative in a narrative sense, but a period of time between the moment he was getting ready and the moment he was about to shoot. So, it was a Marcel Proust thing, almost—memories or images flowing through.

When my father was using the camera he would just pick it up and shoot, never framing it by the eye. For many years he brought the 8 millimeter camera with him everywhere. What's really interesting while watching the Rolling Stones here is that, at the time, Toni Basil was a close friend of the family and invited us to go to the dress rehearsals for the *T.A.M.I. Show*. For those of you who don't know the *T.A.M.I. Show*, it was the first live-concert movie of an actual concert. It was like a variety show, but a magnificent variety show where you got to see the Miracles, the Stones, Chuck Berry, Gerry and the Pacemakers—the best band of them all, of course.

Andrew Lampert

James Brown.

TB James Brown, a legendary James Brown performance.

So my father and I went to the dress rehearsals at the Santa Monica Civic, I think it was late morning, and my dad had his camera with him. At the time there were no restrictions about somebody coming in with a camera, or there were no concerns about it—he could have shot everything if he wanted to. They did not know he was going to bring a camera; that was always a part of his body, in a sense. We met the Rolling Stones, I met Mick Jagger, and we watched the Supremes rehearse. The Beach Boys came on afterwards, and they actually wore the striped shirts and the white pants. It was interesting seeing the Supremes' Motown in a funky moment with hair curlers, the Beach Boys were totally hardcore Beach Boy, and the Stones were the Stones.

The interesting thing is that my dad shot the footage of the Stones from a movie screen. We went to the Bruin Theatre, or the Fox, he brought his camera and shot it from the third row. He could have actually shot it right there and then in front of them, but he chose the distance of having a film in between them. That always strikes me as a really important aspect of my dad's work—that all the images are secondhand images from publications like *Look* and *Life* magazine. During that time, the sixties and afterwards, news-photo magazines were a huge deal. My father collected news magazines, but he didn't collect them for just anything—he wasn't interested in getting *Life* magazine from 1943, he was into the issue from the moment he was working in. So anything you see from the past, like Hitler or Mussolini, was not *Life* magazine or *Look* magazine from the forties, it was reprinted in a 1966 *Life* magazine article about the war, or war years.

He shot whenever he felt like shooting something. It's an interesting film because, though he didn't shoot the Stones in person, there are people from our house. It was mostly shot in Beverly Glen, which is the area between UCLA, Sunset Boulevard, and Coldwater Canyon. We lived in a one-room shack with stilts looking over Beverly Glen. It was very small, and my memory of it is ongoing guests 24/7, until my dad became more of a private person.

AW So what about *View* magazine?

TB *View* magazine was a huge thing for my father. It was published by Charles Henri Ford in New York; his time is associated with the surrealists. All those heroes in exile who lived in New York contributed greatly, like Duchamp, Man Ray, I think even Picabia. My dad collected it at the time it was being issued; he had a complete collection, and it had a really profound effect on him. Unfortunately, his mother, my grandmother, threw the entire collection away.

AW And the comics—that was the most intense story in your book.

TB Yeah, that's horrifying. I'm sweating right now, because of the memories.

I collected comic books as a child, and it was a serious collection. If I had number one and I had number three, I'd better have number two. So I had this comic book collection and I kept it up for some years, and then one day I came home and I went to my precious comic book collection, just to enjoy the essence of my collection, really not even to look at the covers. I kept the comic books in stacks or in drawers; I didn't have a bookshelf or anything else. I looked at the top comic, which was usually the latest one of mostly Marvel Comics, and I noticed on the cover it said "collector's item," but handstamped. And I looked at the one underneath, "collector's item," and I'm trying to figure this out—how? why? what? Then I took, like, four at a time: "collector's item." And then I went to the bottom of the pile: "collector's item." It was getting to be like a *Twilight Zone*–intensity fear thing, so I thought I had some magazine sort of hidden underneath the bed in my drawer, so I opened the drawer to look at those comic books: "collector's item." Then under the bed: "collector's item." Now I'm in a panic because it's crazy that somehow every comic book I have is handstamped "collector's item." So I went downstairs to see my father, he was reading the newspaper, and he's facing the other way. I walked down and said, "Dad, I have to tell you that there's something really strange happening right now and I have to talk to you about this." So I tapped him on the shoulder, he faced me, and on his forehead it said "collector's item."

AW It's terrifying, unsettling, but so funny.

AL Really crazy story.

AW And what did you do?

TB I think I screamed; I definitely screamed.

But after that I didn't keep my comic book collection, I gave it up. And there's two ways of looking at this: Wallace and I never had a son-and-father discussion or talk—in fact we didn't talk at all. I'd been with him every day for almost twenty-one years, until he died, and we never actually talked about stuff. It was mostly helping him work and being in his presence. But many years later, thinking about it and hearing the story about *View* magazine, which his mother got rid of, it's sort of a similar thing. At first it's very funny. My dad had a duality in humor. One is the absurdity of it. And then, two, it's kind of mean.

AW But it's layered and it's mysterious.

TB Very mysterious, and he never explained why he did it. And I didn't ask him, because I was taught to accept things. I don't want to say "taught" because in that environment, and especially in a bohemian landscape, you just sort of accept things as they happen, without any judgment. I was taught, or learned, not to pass judgment on life as it was in front of me. But the stamp was only on my comic books, which were so precious to me that I could die.

AW But whether he had it made in particular for that, or . . . ?

TB I think he actually bought it commercial because it wasn't that the stamp itself was unusual, it was the fact that it was a handheld stamp and it was on my property.

AW And he had to do it again and again.

TB Well, he did a lot of stuff like that, I think it might have been in the book. We were very close friends with Russ Tamblyn, the actor and a known artist. Wallace, Russell, and I went to the opening of *Pink Flamingos* at the Nuart Theatre, so it was like '72, '73, and Russ, who knows George Maharis, who's an actor in *Route 66*, was the person who sort of presented *Pink Flamingos*.

AW & AL Really?

TB Yes, it's very interesting. It was like a "this is my people" type of thing. And Russell was totally blown away, saying, "I can't believe that George Maharis is gay," and Wallace is going, "Uh-huh, uh-huh"—he was sort of blown away by the fact that somebody he knew was actually gay, and knew the *Pink Flamingos* world at the time. He wouldn't be that way now. At the same time, there was a new publication out called *Playgirl* and the first pinup of *Playgirl* is George Maharis. It's him standing by a Corvette because of *Route 66*, naked, covering himself with the open car door. So my dad bought *Playgirl*, he cut it very carefully, had it framed, and wrote, "To Russ with great love. Thank you for the night, love, George." Now, the deliberate part of that, besides that, is he broke into Russ's house in the night while they were sleeping, took the artwork from the mantelpiece down, and put that framed photograph of George Maharis on the mantelpiece. So my dad came back the next day, and the next day afterward, and the George Maharis photograph was there; Russell did not even notice.

AL I'm not sure that story made the book.

TB That didn't make the book?

AL That might be exclusive content.

AW I'm just curious about his relationship to film, and the making of this film and his connection to all these people working in film and in Hollywood and so on—it seems like a slightly different world or layer, maybe not irrelevant, somehow. How did his film go over with his contemporaries?

TB I think in the forties—I'm not a historian, so keep that in mind—in the forties, there was a place in Los Angeles called the Coronet Theatre that showed underground films.

AL Raymond Rohauer. He had the theater, but he was also a distributor, so he is one of the earliest distributors on a big scale of experimental cinema and international cinema as well.

TB And Buster Keaton movies.

AL And Buster Keaton. Rohauer was one of the early "film pirates," somebody who got old films that were public domain, or where copyrights had lapsed, or where there were only a few prints. He made new copies, he put his name on them and claimed ownership, but he was an incredibly valuable person to film culture.

TB As a young man, my dad and my mom often did date nights—actually my dad met my mom there, at the Coronet Theatre, when they were showing *Blood of a Poet* by Cocteau. But my dad would go there on a regular basis, he was a regular filmgoer, with people in the audience like D. W. Griffith, which is kind of interesting. D. W. Griffith was a regular customer at this theater. But yeah, he liked narrative, mainstream films. They really, really loved artists' films, or films from the underground cinema, or art films in the world of Jonas Mekas and early Warhol and people like that.

AL Russ Tamblyn and Dean Stockwell, who you see here, are part of that interesting circuit of child stars who were younger than Wallace and fell under his spell. Did he bring these worlds together by showing works by Brakhage or Bruce Conner and other people in the film art world to his friends who were more in the industry?

TB Yes, but not in an organized way—this is actually an important point to make. My dad showed his films in standard 8 millimeter and had an 8 millimeter projector. He never showed the film like what we're seeing now, in front of an audience or a large audience—mostly one-to-one or two or three people, and it was usually people who came to the studio or to our house. It would be very casual, like, "Do you want to see my film?" He would show it on a refrigerator door, or a space on the wall; it's a small image because it's 8 millimeter. It was like *Semina*, which is a publication that he published and hand-made. He gave *Semina* to people directly or mailed it to people; it was never sold on the open market or to a bookstore. He had no concern about distribution of *Semina* and, like *Semina*, he had no interest in distributing what is known as *Aleph*.

He had a list of people he admired, and he would send to those people. And then he also gave it to personal friends. There was Russ from MGM Studios, Judy Garland, Dean Stockwell, Elizabeth Taylor, they all went to school together and they were raised and played together. And the weird thing, I think—in most cases, generally speaking, is that they had damaged childhoods. They were not happy people in that environment. Dean and Russ both dropped out from acting numerous times, and they are the ones with really good, long film careers and ups and downs, but did a lot of interesting work throughout their lives. But when Dean and Russell met my father, he gave them permission to do other things and make their own movies, because they didn't make their own films or do their own art. He was definitely the one person who said, "Yeah, you can do this or you can just go with it," and they needed that encouragement.

AL I think it may be helpful to explain a little about the film for a second. It is shot on regular 8 millimeter, which is actually 8 millimeters wide. It's very small, with little holes called "sprockets" that run along the side. The projector that he's referring to is an 8 millimeter projector, a little tabletop machine. When editing film, which is also called splicing, you cut it, take this part and that part, put them together and use glue or tape to join the two parts. As the film's passing through the machine, there's little teeth that engage with the sprockets and this is what pushes the film through the projector. But, when you have splices, they tend to jump, so you have to be really good at making a splice, and let's just say that Wallace was okay at making a splice.

TB He's one of the best okays in the business.

AL A high okay.

While projecting the film, there could be technical problems. The footage that he shot and projected, time and time again, is the original. It's not a copy. It's not a negative, it's positive. Think of it like shooting a Polaroid, and you have the original picture. That's what he had. So he edited that, he cut it into pieces, very small pieces, as you can tell from the machine-gun nature of it. He also drew on it, painted on it, and added Letraset, which is this old sort of press-on type used for graphics and layout. It, for sure, makes the film thicker and more capable of burning up. He worked on *Aleph* for ten years, so part of that is the editing of the image, as well as literally adding stuff onto the film itself. When you have the film and you're editing, you sit at a table and the film is on reels held by these little arms. You wind through, you have a little splicer, and you make your cuts. You can read the Letraset, numbers, letters, actual words that he laid on it, but when the film is projected all this visual information is going the other direction. It's visible as part of the image, but it isn't really decipherable. When you watch the film, there's many ways to watch it.

Aleph moves at eighteen frames per second. That's eighteen individual images per second, and there can be as many as three or four cuts sometimes happening in this second, because he's doing one or two or three frames. It's completely rapid-fire. As Tosh was saying, he would invite you over and show you the film and the film would then stop—the projector would stop working, or burst into flame, or would start shredding off the sprockets which are necessary for it to be projected. He would stop the projector, rip off or take out the ruined material, make a splice, put it back together, and just keep going. The damaged footage was edited out. I wrote something about it once; I described it as editing by attrition instead of addition—it's what can get through the projector.

When he passed away, I think your mother told me this story, somebody came up to the door at your place unannounced and said that Jonas Mekas had sent them for the film. And she said, "Excuse me?" "Jonas Mekas in New York has sent me for the film." Some years earlier, Jonas had gotten your father a year-long grant from a philanthropist and filmmaker named Jerome Hill, who used Jonas as his secret agent to distribute helpful grants to underground experimental filmmakers. So Jonas, in his infinite wisdom, having never seen the film but having heard of it, got Wallace enough money so that he did not have to be the garbageman of Topanga for a year.

TB Paid off car payments with that, yes.

AL And then, after Wallace dies, the man shows up wanting the film for Jonas—it's like the godfather needs the film. And she didn't give it to him. But then somehow or other she passed the film on to Stan Brakhage, and Brakhage took the film to a laboratory and had an 8 millimeter copy made. He made a copy of it, it's another positive from the positive, and from that a few 8 millimeter prints were made, one of which resided in Anthology. In the early nineties, Brakhage took this copy of a copy and blew it up to 16 millimeter so that it could be distributed at the Film-Makers' Co-op and Canyon Cinema in California. And then in the early 2000s, I asked Tosh what the status was with the preservation of the film, and it was so confusing that Tosh said, "I don't know, but there's some boxes here," and he sent them to me.

I found the original that Brakhage had copied in a can that had an Aleph on it. The Anthology preservation I made was the result of working directly from the original, so it's closer to the source. We made a new preservation that's an optical blow-up. In the process of doing that, I found, in this box that Tosh had sent, that there were other 8 millimeter films. There was an 8 millimeter film by Bruce Conner, there was an 8 millimeter film by Russ Tamblyn. There were also cigar boxes filled with spaghetti—because that's really what 8 millimeter film looks like. None of it had sprockets, it was all damaged. It turned out that there's another twenty-eight minutes or so of what at one point was *Aleph*. It wasn't cut out because it didn't work narratively, or because the scene was too long. He simply couldn't project it anymore.

AW Did you keep the artifact?

AL Oh yeah. There were a few films. There's a 16 millimeter film that Paul Beattie shot of George Herms and Edmund Teske's exhibit on a houseboat dock at the Semina Gallery that Berman ran. Was it a one-day show?

TB My dad had his own gatherings in Larkspur in a burnt-out structure. They had no roof, hardly any flooring, mold everywhere, and if you even walked there, you would have to go on these boardwalks. So he would have these shows that would last about two hours on a Saturday and that was it.

AL There's lovely footage of this one show with little Tosh and other kids running around, and then there is another reel that is Wallace riding a motorcycle, shot by Dean Stockwell. And then there's something like twenty-eight minutes more of *Aleph*. All of this was repaired and preserved in a film that we call *Artifactual: Films from the Wallace Berman Collection*. The film includes a lot of careful introductory wording to say that the content is edited by him, but we organized it; we did this.

So that's the background that informs *Aleph*'s material history.

AW I was going to ask about the issue of time—you feel it has a beginning, middle?

TB I do, yes.

AW But was that narratively, within the time it was shot? Are the last shots the later shots? What are the noticeable jumps in time, leaps in time?

TB Well, there's no proof of this, but I think my dad had seen *Blood of a Poet* not long before filming. In the beginning you see the tower, and then towards the end you see the tower collapse. I'm gonna take a wild guess that the footage had stuck in his brain; I think he was a really big Cocteau lover. But I feel it's pretty hard for me to talk about the film objectively, because there's so many people I know in the movie, so I think of people who are or are no longer here.

AL This is your home movie.

TB It is a home movie of sorts, but at the same time it is clearly not a home movie. So it's kind of difficult, because really the film represents my dad's life. It has an optimistic thing going through it, but there's also darkness. Definitely the narcotics theme contributes to that darkness. I know my father and Bob Alexander had a rocky relationship due to Bob's devotion to heroin. And again, my father's not judgmental on narcotics or drugs, but it definitely had an effect on his own lifestyle, and I think he was concerned about me being in that world and that landscape as well. But there's so much of my dad's personal life in there, and all his passions—the dancing sequences. The film is almost like a dance film to me—my father as a teenager was a zoot suit jazz-loving Los Angeles toughie. He went to a lot of jazz clubs in his teenage years, and he did try [Charlie] Parker's recording for Dial Records—he did the album cover of that as a teenager. He was also a champion swing dancer with his girlfriend at the time. I think his love of dance or movement has never changed. He loved ballet, but he actually never went to the ballet. I don't think he would ever go to the ballet, but he loved images of ballet dancers. One of his favorite books was Nijinsky's diary. I think he felt that book sort of saved his life, from being a criminal to becoming an artist—that book was like the bridge way. Why? I'm not sure.

AL Have you read it?

TB I have read it; it's a great book by a total lunatic.

AW I guess I'm still curious about his editing—is he going from the resonant moment to the next and propelling forward? Is he going on the energy which is suggested by this dancing and rhythm, or is it a visual resonance? Or more about the kinetic side?

TB To me it's more about dance than kinetics. I feel it's very much intensity of movement. And again, the images of Margot Fonteyn and Nureyev, who was quite a big presence in our life, culturally, because at the time he was like a megastar. My parents, and specifically my dad, really admired him and Margot Fonteyn, and so the dance movements and the love of music is a really big part of this film. And that to me is the pacing of the work.

AW Interesting. Did he listen to music when he worked?

TB Oh, he was listening to music consistently as he worked on this. I should tell you that sometimes when he played the film he would have a soundtrack. He'll play James Brown, "Papa's Got a Brand New Bag." Often he would play the Paul Bowles recordings of Moroccan musicians that he loved, full blast, but he would not do this on a consistent basis. And for my taste, I feel when I'm watching that it's silent. It's really musical to me and John Zorn, a great composer and a great citizen of this world, did a magnificent score for the film, but I have to say, I just prefer it silent. The film is so intense, I don't need anything else—the music in my head or the pacing is enough. It's a pulse.

AL Didn't you say that Brian Jones would come over and look at the film?

TB He had seen it, yes—after the candy show my father became very close to Brian Jones, who was a member of the Rolling Stones at the time. And he would come over to the house quite often when he was in town, which is a lot, and they hung out together. I wish I could give some really important insight here, but they just hung out. They would smoke joints, drink wine, and listen to records. I could tell Brian was at our house because I would be sleeping, as a child, and I'd wake up with a lot of records on the ground.

AL Did you tell me once that Rip Torn came over to the house?

TB He showed Rip Torn the movie on a one-to-one basis. He didn't know him that well—I think Rip was invited by somebody else.

AL It's such an interesting collision of the underground and these actors. What is the story of how you met Russ Tamblyn? He had a big house with a bowling alley in it?

TB Yes, the first time we met him, Dean brought us, all three of us—I used to go to adult parties with my parents. I went to bars with them, everywhere. There's no kiddy time with me really. We were all invited to go to Russ Tamblyn's house. I was very impressed, because I saw *West Side Story*, and I'd seen him recite stories, so I'm like, "Oh my gosh, Russ Tamblyn's house." We go along to Russ Tamblyn's house in Pacific Palisades, and Dean had asked him, "Can I bring my friends Wallace and Shirley Berman?" Russ heard "Shelley Berman," the comedian, so he was expecting Shelley Berman. He opens the door and there's Dean and then there's these ruffians, myself included, Wallace, clearly not Shelley Berman, but Shirley Berman. And what impressed us at the time was Russ was living a very movie-star life. He had a bowling alley downstairs, he had a huge swimming pool, Ping-Pong tables everywhere, awards, you know, pictures and stills from his past films everywhere. And that was his world. Within three months those awards got collaged over, repainted. He shut down the bowling alley to show films by my dad.

AL When I met Russ Tamblyn, he was remembering this and trying to recall the name of a filmmaker he had hosted in person to show his films. And he started describing this very fast-cutting film of people on a vacation in Africa and they're killing the animals and I said, "Peter Kubelka," and he said, "Yes! Peter Kubelka." You almost can't imagine somebody like Russ Tamblyn taking some underground Austrian filmmaker like Peter Kubelka and showing flicker films that cause seizures, and images of animals being mutilated, in the basement of his bowling alley.

Anne, can I ask you, with Wallace and mail art, and this idea of the poetry community and you being in New York, there was a certain overlap of your activities and Wallace's activities—are there comparable figures that you can think of?

AW Well, among the downtown's scene of art, Rudy Burkhardt would send out cards that were collaged. Postcards were really important to the poets then, and it's still a writing exercise that people do—bring out your postcards and share them, and you look at the fine print of the card, and then what's written on it and how you can interfere, cut it up, etc. So that was going on, maybe not in as interesting a way as the *Semina* project, but we were on that list at the Poetry Project. We were doing mimeo, all these magazines and collages. It was very easy to go to people's studios, visual artists, you could just show up, look around or start work, and begin a collaboration. We were always getting covers and things for small editions, and then the magazines—in the sixties I founded *Angel Hair* magazine with Lewis Warsh. That was right after the Berkeley poetry conferences. *Semina* was on our exchange list. We worked with artists such as Tom Brainard, Philip Guston, and others.

If you read up on Duncan and Denise Levertov, they were sending poetry tapes around to each other, recordings, to hear how they sounded where the breath paused. Some tapes disappeared from the Poetry Project archive, but that sense of sending them when only one copy even existed! It was all very innocent. I love the post office still, I always felt it was the only government ally for our work. So that was always great to get some of the stuff, a lot of other small-press little items. Because they're textual but also textile and can be layered and collaged, they become like little time machines—intimate, fragile things that make you think of the journey they've been on and their originals and so on. It was mail art.

AL I feel very satisfied with my life because in 2007, when the Wallace Berman *Semina* show happened at the Grey Art Gallery, you were here for the opening and I got to reintroduce you to your screen father, Taylor Mead.

TB That was very sentimental.

AL Yeah, "Excuse me, Taylor . . . I'd like to introduce you to Tarzan Jr., who played your son in Andy Warhol's *Tarzan and Jane Regained . . . Sort Of.*" The two of you together was a touching moment.

TB What did he say? I can't remember.

AL "Oh. Hi." I think he said "I was great in that movie."

TB Yes, they shot that Warhol *Tarzan and Jane Regained . . . Sort Of* in our house partly.

AL The one that slipped down the hill?

TB Yes, that's a good movie, and an interesting film that really captures the Southern California world at the time.

AL It's also one of the first films of his that's narrative, versus people kissing, or the Empire State Building. So it went from being, your family being friends with child stars to you becoming one.

TB He went to Hollywood to make a Hollywood movie, and he sort of did. It destroyed my acting career though. I could have been a child actor.

Audience member What was the *Easy Rider* role?

TB I was offered a speaking role in *Easy Rider*. Dennis Hopper insisted that my parents be in the movie as extras—he would not take a no, and I went with them as usual. And it's the first time I've been, really, on a—well, no, I've been on TV sets and movie sets before, but not that much. But I like the environment because of the food. I was really into movie catering and food, almost a connoisseur of movie food. So Dennis came to me and said, "Would you like to be in the movie?" And I thought, "Well, all my dad and mom are doing is basically sitting there and you photograph them," so I thought, "Sure." And he tore a script out, like, he had a script with him, and he said, "Here, just learn your lines." So I said, "Yes," and I took it home, that one-page script, and I think it was something like, they pull up to the hippie commune scene, and I was told to run up to Peter Fonda and say, "Welcome," or something.

AL "Hey Daddy."

TB “Hello, Captain.” I tried to remember that line. And really, I couldn’t do it. So I told my parents, “I can’t do this.” They went back the next day without me, because there was more commune stuff to shoot, and they told Dennis. He had no problem with it. It was no problem.

AL Your parents were also extras in the adaptation of Jack Kerouac’s novel *The Subterraneans.*

TB Yes, I wrote about the actress who’s in it, Leslie Caron. Legend is that for them to do this extra scene, they convinced Leslie Caron that she must babysit me for one night. And apparently she did—so John Wieners, Leslie Caron . . .

AL And Cameron, who was the highest priestess of the dark arts.

TB Cameron’s the ultimate of the ultimates of every ultimate thing you can ultimately be involved in. Right now there’s such a strong interest in Cameron’s work and in her life—she was married to Jack Parsons. And my parents were invited to their house by another person who was into the occult. They were heavily into occult at that time, famous for it. Jack Parsons by daytime was a genius rocket scientist, but then at nighttime was heavily into the Aleister Crowley world, like worked under him in a sense. So it’s a party for his fellow scientists, my mom was there and of course my dad, and there’s only, like, weirdos at this party full of scientists. And Cameron sees my parents and is like, “I’m gonna associate with these people.” So they became very close friends, and Cameron became one of the covers of *Semina*. She had a profound effect on my father later, and for the Ferus art gallery show, which has been told many, many times over.

Audience member Is there any reason to think that he was aware of Len Lye?

AL I would imagine that, if he was watching films of that era, like *A Colour Box* or *The Birth of the Robot*, especially if he was going to the Coronet Theatre with Rohauer, that he would have had some exposure to those films. And within communities in San Francisco, Len Lye was showing in the art and cinema series that Frank Stauffacher was running, so I think so. Brakhage for sure seems to be more of a corollary kind of figure, in terms of also being under the influence of so many people, with Len Lye included, who were using the filmstrip as painting. The original of *Aleph*, to me, is a sculpture that you wind through, and the unfortunate thing is that every act of viewing it is an act of destruction—that’s the essence of the medium. The only other film that I personally handled that had that same feeling, of holding a sculpture instead of just a print or a copy, is Carolee Schneemann’s *Fuses*. Everything that could be attached to that thing was taped onto it, and it’s remarkable as you wind through it because you have to hold your hand underneath to make sure things aren’t falling out.

Audience member There’s no title on the film—how did you deduce it was called *Aleph*?

TB My father never used a proper title for the film. After he died, which Andy sort of brought up, an aleph was on the tin can, and Stan Brakhage felt very strongly that it should be titled *Aleph*.* I was torn, thinking, "My dad didn't call it anything, so maybe I should be true to the spirit and not call it . . . ," but that is totally impractical, and very much more impractical in the world we live in. And so, *Aleph* became the official title, mostly because Stan Brakhage put the idea in my head that it should be called *Aleph*. But yes, my father had names. I think he had *Aleph* for a little bit in the beginning of making the film, but then he dropped the title and didn't think about it.

---

* Aleph, or א, is the first letter in the Hebrew alphabet.

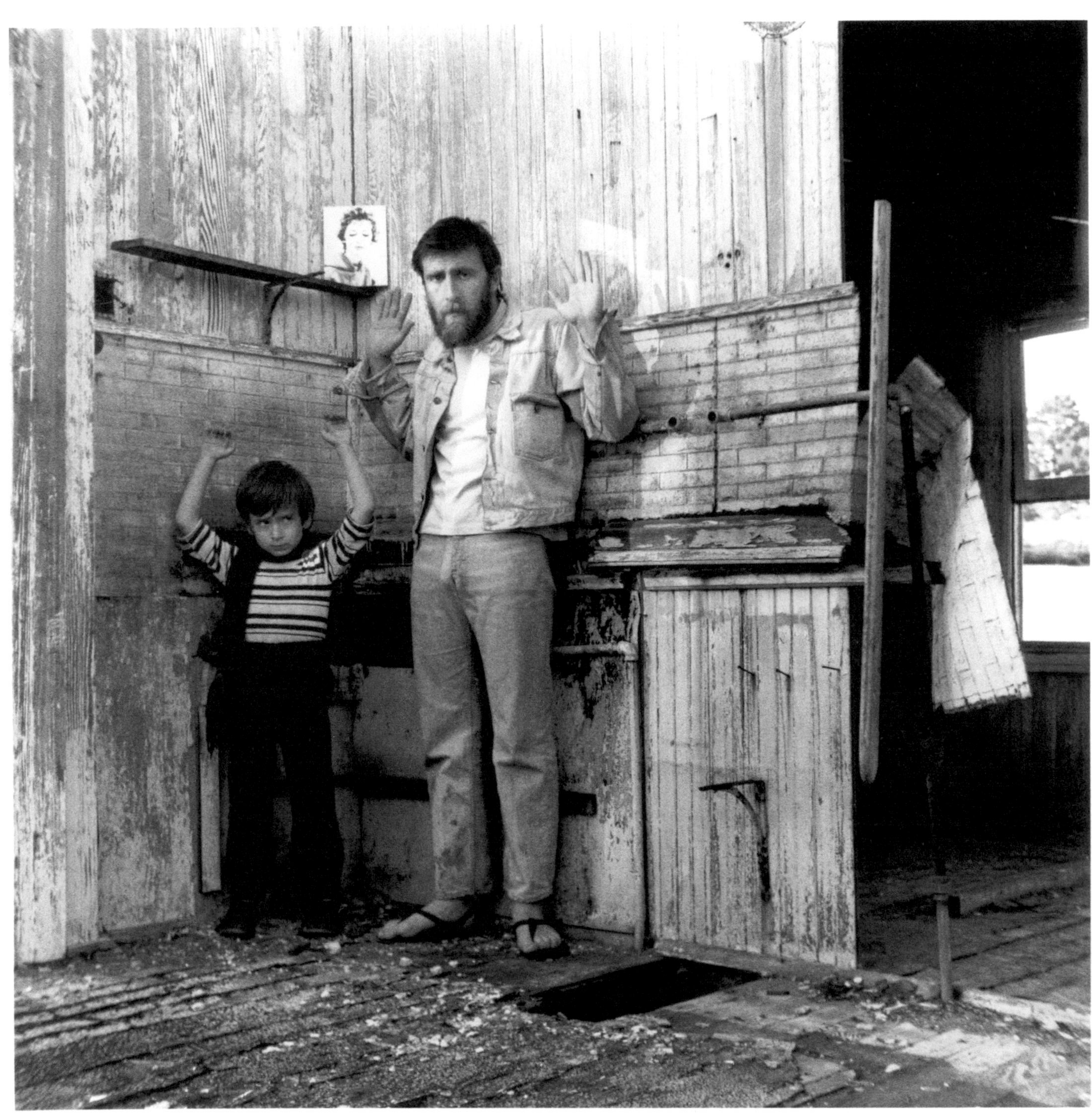

LIST OF WORKS

Untitled, c. 1968
Verifax collage
37.25 × 33 inches (94.5 × 83.5 cm)

Untitled (Mandala with Aleph Center, Mushroom Below), c. 1965
negative Verifax collage
10 × 8.5 inches (25.5 × 21.5 cm)

Untitled (Ray Charles, This Is the Card That Reads 7), c. 1965
collage
12.5 × 8.5 inches (31.75 × 21.5 cm)

Untitled (Proof, Yalta and Broads in Beige), c. 1965
Verifax collage with proof stamp
5 × 7.5 inches (12.70 × 19 cm)

Untitled, 1964–76
acrylic, Verifax collage, and transfer lettering on board
13 × 10.25 inches (33 × 26 cm)

Untitled (Business Man at Desk), c. 1965
Verifax collage
7 × 7 inches (17.75 × 17.75 cm)

Untitled (Moonscape with 3 Arrows), 1964–76
Verifax collage with writing
18.25 × 9 inches (46.5 × 21 cm)

Untitled (Louis Armstrong/Syringe in mouth), 1946
print
13 × 11.25 inches (33 × 28.5 cm)

Untitled, 1964–76
Four-part negative Verifax collage
13 × 14 inches (33.02 × 35.56 cm)

Untitled (C3-Cross), c. 1975
Twenty-five-part negative Verifax collage
33.5 × 30.5 inches (85 × 77.5 cm)

Untitled #129, 1976
single Verifax collage with acrylic
6 × 6.5 inches (15.25 × 16.5 cm)

Untitled #125, c. 1964–76
single Verifax collage with acrylic
6 × 6.5 inches (15.25 × 16.5 cm)

Untitled #126, c. 1964–76
single Verifax collage with acrylic
6 × 6.5 inches (15.25 × 16.5 cm)

Untitled #120, c. 1964–76
single negative Verifax collage
6 × 6.5 inches (15 × 16.5 cm)

Untitled (Faceless Faces with Kabbalah), 1963
paint on photograph mounted on board with hand-applied varnish
34 × 30 inches (86.5 × 76 cm)

Untitled (Office Management), 1964
Verifax collage on book page
10 × 7.75 inches (25.5 × 19.5 cm)

Untitled (A1-Jet), 1964–76
Four-part positive Verifax collage
13 × 14 inches (33 × 35.5 cm)

Untitled (A1-Nebulae), 1964–76
Four-part negative Verifax collage
13 × 14 inches (33 × 35.5 cm)

Untitled, 1964–76
Four-part negative Verifax collage
13 × 14 inches (33 × 35.5 cm)

Untitled, 1964–76
Four-part positive Verifax collage
13 × 14 inches (33 × 35.5 cm)

Untitled, 1956–57
woodstain and ink on parchment on canvas
19.5 × 19.5 inches (49.5 × 49.5 cm)

Untitled (Odd Couple Red Background), 1970
collage
6.25 × 5 inches (16 × 13 cm)

Untitled (Jack Ruby), 1964
photograph with handwritten poem
28.5 × 29 inches (72.5 × 73.5 cm)

Untitled (Insert in "Semina" 7), 1961
offset lithograph from the *Semina* facsimile
4.75 × 3.75 inches (12 × 9.5 cm)

Untitled, c. 1965
Nine-part positive Verifax collage
18 × 20 inches (45.75 × 51 cm)

Untitled #58, c. 1964–76
single negative Verifax collage
6 × 6.5 inches (15 × 16.5 cm)

Untitled #128, c. 1964–76
single Verifax collage with acrylic
6 × 6.5 inches (15.25 × 16.5 cm)

Untitled #82, c. 1964–76
single negative Verifax collage
6 × 6.5 inches (15 × 16.5 cm)

Untitled #109, c. 1964–76
single negative Verifax collage
6 × 6.5 inches (15 × 16.5 cm)

Untitled #102, c. 1964–76
single negative Verifax collage
6 × 6.5 inches (15 × 16.5 cm)

Untitled #21, c. 1964–76
single negative Verifax collage
6 × 6.5 inches (15 × 16.5 cm)

Untitled #7, c. 1964–76
single negative Verifax collage
6 × 6.5 inches (15 × 16.5 cm)

Untitled #123, c. 1964–76
single Verifax collage with acrylic
6 × 6.5 inches (15.25 × 16.5 cm)

Untitled #86, c. 1964–76
single negative Verifax collage
6 × 6.5 inches (15 × 16.5 cm)

Untitled #119, c. 1964–76
single negative Verifax collage
6 × 6.5 inches (15 × 16.5 cm)

Untitled #79, c. 1964–76
single negative Verifax collage
6.5 × 6.5 inches (16.5 × 16.5 cm)

Untitled #40, c. 1964–76
single negative Verifax collage
6 × 6.5 inches (15 × 16.5 cm)

Radio Aether, 1966–1974
box of thirteen offset lithographs of the Verifax series printed on Starwhite cover, mounted on Gemini Ragboard
12.25 × 14.25 inches (31 × 36 cm)
Edition 21 of 50

Untitled (Semina Gallery), 1961
modern inkjet print
20 × 16 inches (51 × 40.5 cm)

Untitled (Two ton rock, two seals), c. 1964–76
polaroid transfer on magazine map
5 × 3.5 inches (13 × 9 cm)

Untitled (Booster Bng), 1967
offset poster, published by John Martin
25 × 22 inches (63.50 × 56 cm)

Untitled (Retard Para), 1965
offset poster
21 × 17 inches (53 × 43 cm)

Untitled (2nd Annual LA Filmmakers Festival), c. 1963
offset poster
20 × 16 inches (51 × 40.5 cm)

Aleph, 1956–66
16mm film transferred to video (black-and-white, silent)

Untitled (Tosh and Wallace Berman at Semina Gallery in Larkspur, CA), 1961
contemporary silver gelatin print
10 × 8 inches (25.5 × 20 cm)

Untitled (Wallace Berman at Semina Gallery, Larkspur, CA), 1961
contemporary silver gelatin print
8 × 10 inches (20 × 25.5 cm)

WALLACE BERMAN

Wallace Berman (born 1926, Staten Island) refined his artistic vision in California from the 1950s to the '70s, living in San Francisco then Los Angeles, cultivating a like-minded community, and eschewing academic constraints. His critical involvement with the Beat Generation and contribution to the art and culture of that region was influential but largely forgotten by the mainstream art-consuming public. His mail-art folio *Semina* was self-published from 1955 to '64 and has become an iconic chronicle of emerging thinkers and writers from the era. A complete catalogue of *Semina* editions is now included in the Archives of American Art, Smithsonian Institution.

In 2016, Kohn Gallery, Los Angeles, staged *American Aleph*, the first comprehensive retrospective of the artist in nearly forty years. Solo exhibitions have also taken place at the Whitney Museum of American Art, New York (1978), and the Santa Monica Museum of Art (2007). Today, Berman's works are held in the collections of the Centre Pompidou, Paris; the Tate Modern, London; the Museum of Modern Art, New York; the Whitney Museum of American Art, New York; the Los Angeles County Museum of Art; and the Museum of Contemporary Art, Los Angeles, among many others. Berman died in a car accident on his fiftieth birthday, February 18, 1976, in Topanga Canyon, California.

SELECTED SOLO EXHIBITIONS

2021 TOTAH, New York, NY, *Off the Grid*

2016 Kohn Gallery, Los Angeles, CA, *American Aleph*

2010 Galerie Frank Elbaz, Paris, France, *Wallace Berman: Be-bop Kabbalah*

Anne Mosseri-Marlio Galerie, Zurich, Switzerland, *Wallace Berman – Verifax*

2009 Nicole Klagsbrun Gallery, New York, NY, *Wallace Berman, 1927–1976*

2008 Camden Art Centre, London, UK, *All Is Personal: The Art of Wallace Berman*

2005 The Jewish Museum, New York, NY, *Aleph: A Film by Wallace Berman*

2000 Musée d'Art Moderne et Contemporain, Geneva, Switzerland, *Art Is Love Is God, une introduction, 1957–1976*

1992 ICA/Amsterdam, Amsterdam, Netherlands, *Wallace Berman: Support the Revolution*

1990 Louver Gallery, New York, NY, *Wallace Berman: A Gesture Involving Verifax Collage, Photographs, Text and Sculpture*

1988 L.A. Louver, Venice, CA, *Works from the Estate*

1982 Charles Cowles Gallery, New York, NY, *Wallace Berman*

1979 L.A. Louver, Venice, CA, *Works by Wallace Berman: Art Is Love Is God*

L.A. Louver, Venice, CA, *Wallace Berman*

1978 Otis Art Institute, Los Angeles, CA (traveled to Fort Worth Art Museum, Fort Worth, TX; University Art Museum, Berkeley, CA; Seattle Art Museum, Seattle, WA), *Wallace Berman Retrospective* (catalogue)

Whitney Museum of American Art, New York, NY, *Wallace Berman*

1977 Timothea Stewart Gallery, Los Angeles, CA, *Wallace Berman*

1974 Gemini G.E.L., Los Angeles, CA, *Radio/Aether Series*

1973 Mermaid Tavern, Topanga, CA

1968 Los Angeles County Museum of Art, Los Angeles, CA (catalogue), *Wallace Berman*

The Jewish Museum, New York, NY (catalogue), *Wallace Berman: Verifax Collages*

1967 Topanga Community House, Topanga, CA

1965 Studio Exhibition, Beverly Glen Canyon, Los Angeles, CA

1957 Ferus Gallery, Los Angeles, CA

SELECTED GROUP EXHIBITIONS

2017 The Metropolitan Museum of Art, New York, NY, *Delirious: Art at the Limits of Reason 1950–1980*

Simon Lee Gallery, London, UK, *Screen Memory*

2016 The Menil Collection, Houston, Texas; Nicole Klagsbrun, New York, NY, *Holy Barbarians: Beat Culture on the West Coast*

Norton Simon Museum, Pasadena, CA, *Duchamp to Pop*

2015 Kohn Gallery, Los Angeles, CA, *The West Coast Avant-Garde: 1950–Present*

2014 Eldridge Street Synagogue, New York, NY, *Walls and Words* (organized by UNTITLED Gallery)

2013 Crocker Art Museum, Sacramento, CA (traveled to Grey Art Gallery, New York University, NY; Katzen Arts Center, American University, Washington DC; Pasadena Museum of California Art, Pasadena, CA), *An Opening of the Field: Jess, Robert Duncan, and Their Circle* (curated by Michael Duncan)

2012 Michael Kohn Gallery, Los Angeles, CA, *Into the Mystic*

Pasadena Museum of California Art, Pasadena, CA, *L.A. Raw: Abject Expressionism in Los Angeles 1945–1980* (curated by Michael Duncan)

Martin-Gropius-Bau, Berlin, Germany, *Pacific Standard Time: Art in L.A. 1950–1980*

2011 Getty Center, Los Angeles, CA, *Pacific Standard Time: Art in L.A. 1945–1980*

Palais de Tokyo, Paris, France, *All of the Above: Carte Blanche à John M. Armleder*

The Armory Center, Pasadena, CA, *Speaking in Tongues: Wallace Berman and Robert Heinecken, 1961–1976* (curated by Claudia Bohn-Spector and Sam Mellon)

Michael Kohn Gallery, Los Angeles, CA, *25th Anniversary Show*

2009 Foundation 20 21 / Nyehaus, New York, NY, *California Maximalism: Sticking a Spike into the Vein of Memory*

Michael Kohn Gallery, Los Angeles, CA, *She: Images of Women by Wallace Berman and Richard Prince*

2008 Moderna Museet, Stockholm, Sweden, *Time & Place: Los Angeles 1957–1968*

Museum Ludwig, Cologne, Germany, *Looking for Mushrooms: Beat Poets, Hippies, Funk, Minimal Art, San Francisco 1955–1968*

Centre Pompidou, Paris, France, *Trace du Sacré*

2007 CCA Wattis Institute for Contemporary Arts, San Francisco, CA, *Pioneers*

2006 CCA Wattis Institute for Contemporary Arts, San Francisco, CA, *Radical Software—Art, Technology, and the Bay Area Underground*

Orange County Museum of Art, Newport Beach, CA, *California Modern*

Berkeley Art Museum and Pacific Film Archive, Berkeley, CA, Semina *Culture: Wallace Berman & His Circle*

2005 Andrea Rosen Gallery, New York, NY, *Looking at Words: The Formal Use of Text in Modern and Contemporary Works on Paper*

Santa Monica Museum of Art, Santa Monica, CA (traveled to Nora Eccles Harrison Museum of Art, Logan, UT; Ulrich Museum of Art, Wichita, KS; Berkeley Art Museum and Pacific Film Archive, Berkeley, CA; Grey Art Gallery, New York University, New York, NY), *Semina Culture: Wallace Berman & His Circle*

Patricia Faure Gallery, Santa Monica, CA, *Tony DeLap & Wallace Berman*

2004 The Bronx Museum of the Arts, Bronx, NY, *Subway Series: The New York Yankees and the American Dream*

Whitney Museum of American Art, New York, NY, *Evidence of Impact: Art and Photography 1963–1978*

Bloomberg Space, London, UK, *Collage*

2003 Polk Museum of Art, Lakeland, FL, *Some Assembly Required: Collage Culture in Post-War America*

2002 Gagosian, New York, NY, *Ferus*

2000 Tang Teaching Museum, Saratoga Springs, NY, *S.O.S.: Scenes of Sounds*

1999 Nicole Klagsbrun Gallery, New York, NY, *Group Show*

1998 Santa Monica Museum of Art, Santa Monica, CA, *World Artists for Tibet*

1997 Louisiana Museum of Modern Art, Copenhagen, Denmark, *Sunshine and Noir: Art in Los Angeles 1960–1997*

1992 L.A. Louver, Venice, CA, *Poem Makers: Wallace Berman, George Herms, Jess*

Louver Gallery, New York, NY, *Overlay*

1991 Louver Gallery, New York, NY, *Summer: Scale*

Nicole Klagsbrun Gallery, New York, NY, *Wallace Berman, Bruce Conner, Jay DeFeo, George Herms, Jess*

1990 L.A. Louver, Venice, CA, *Contemporary Assemblage: The Dada and Surrealist Legacy*

Milwaukee Art Museum, Milwaukee, WI, *Words as Image: American Art 1960–1990*

1989 California State University, Hayward, CA (traveled to Richard Reynolds Gallery, University of the Pacific, Stockton, CA), *Collage/Assemblage: Nine Points of View*

Whitney Museum of American Art at Equitable Center, New York, NY, *The "Junk" Aesthetic: Assemblage of the 1950s and Early 1960s*

Wight Art Gallery, UCLA, Los Angeles, CA (traveled to Fresno Art Museum, Fresno, CA; Blaffer Gallery, University of Houston, Houston, TX; Joslyn Art Museum, Omaha, NE) (catalogue), *Forty Years of California Assemblage*

Newport Harbor Art Museum, Newport Beach, CA (traveled to Henry Art Gallery, Seattle, WA; Palm Springs Desert Museum, Palm Springs, CA; Wadsworth Atheneum, Wadsworth, CT; Neuberger Museum, Purchase, NY; Phoenix Art Museum, Phoenix, AZ), *LA Pop in the Sixties*

1988 Herron Gallery, Indianapolis, IL, *The Art of George Herms and Wallace Berman*

James Corcoran Gallery, Santa Monica, CA, and G. Ray Hawkins Gallery, Los Angeles, CA (catalogue), *Lost and Found in California: Four Decades of Assemblage Art*

Hirshhorn Museum and Sculpture Garden, Washington DC (catalogue), *Different Drummers*

San Antonio Museum of Art, San Antonio, TX (traveled to Boise Art Museum, Boise, ID; Art Museum of South Texas, Corpus Christi, TX; Amarillo Art Center, Amarillo, TX), *Poetic Objects*

1987 Kent Fine Art, Inc., New York, NY (catalogue), *Assemblage*

1986 L.A. Louver, Venice, CA, *American/European Painting and Sculpture 1986. Part 1*

1985 College of Notre Dame, Belmont, CA, *Past Presence / Contemporary Sources*

San Francisco Museum of Modern Art, San Francisco, CA, *The Twentieth Century: The San Francisco Museum of Modern Art Collection*

1983 Gallery Paule Anglim, San Francisco, CA, *Sight Vision: The Urban Milieu*

1982 Santa Monica College Art Gallery, Santa Monica, CA, *The Peace Show*

Contemporary Arts Museum, Houston, TX, *The Americans: The Collage*

1981 L.A. Louver, Venice, CA, *Group Show: California: A Sense of Individualism: Part I*

Los Angeles County Museum of Art, Los Angeles, CA (traveled to San Antonio Museum of Art, San Antonio, TX), *Art in Los Angeles: Seventeen Artists in the Sixties*

Laguna Beach Museum of Art, Laguna, CA, *Southern California Artists: 1940–1980*

1980 L.A. Louver, Venice, CA, *Group Show: Summer Exhibition Part I*

1979 International Museum of Photography at George Eastman House, New York, NY, *Electroworks*

1977 San Francisco Museum of Modern Art, San Francisco, CA (traveled to Smithsonian Institution, Washington, DC), *Painting and Sculpture in California: The Modern Era*

1976 Newport Harbor Art Museum, Newport Beach, CA, *The Last Time I Saw Ferus: 1957–1966*

1975 Los Angeles Institute of Contemporary Art, Los Angeles, CA, *Collage and Assemblage*

Memorial Union Art Gallery, University of California, Davis, CA, *Environment and the New Art: 1960–1975*

John and Norah Warbeke Gallery, Mount Holyoke College, South Hadley, MA, *Art as a Muscular Principle: 10 Artists and San Francisco, 1950–1965*

1974 Dallas Museum of Fine Arts, Dallas, TX (traveled to San Francisco Museum of Art, San Francisco, CA; Wadsworth Atheneum, Hartford, CT), *Poets of the Cities: New York and San Francisco, 1950–1965*

1969 Pasadena Art Museum, Pasadena, CA (traveled to City Art Museum of St. Louis, St. Louis, MO; Art Gallery of Ontario, Toronto, Canada; Fort Worth Art Center Museum, Fort Worth, TX), *West Coast, 1945–1969*

Hayward Gallery, London, UK, *Pop Art Redefined*

1968 University of California, Irvine, CA (catalogue), *Assemblage in California*

1966 Robert Fraser Gallery, London, UK (catalogue), *Los Angeles Now*

PUBLICATIONS

2016 Claudia Bohn-Spector and Sam Mellon, eds., *Wallace Berman: American Aleph*, Kohn Gallery, 2016

2015 Michael Duncan and Kristine McKenna, eds., *Semina Culture: Wallace Berman & His Circle*, D.A.P. / Santa Monica Museum of Art, February 24, 2015

2014 Johan Kugelberg, ed., *Semina 1955–1964: Art Is Love Is God*, Boo-Hooray, March 31, 2014

1993 Tosh Berman, *Wallace Berman: Support the Revolution*, Institute of Contemporary Art, 1993

1964 *Semina 9*, Self-published

1963 *Semina 8*, Self-published

1961 *Semina 7*, Self-published

1960 *Semina VI*, Self-published

1959 *Semina 5*, Self-published

Semina 4, Self-published

1958 *Semina 3*, Self-published

1957 *Semina Two*, Self-published

1955 *Semina 1*, Self-published

SELECTED COLLECTIONS

Berardo Collection Museum, Collection of Modern and Contemporary Art, Lisbon, Portugal

Corcoran Gallery of Art, Washington, DC

Fotomuseum Winterthur, Winterthur, Switzerland

The Jewish Museum, New York, NY

Los Angeles County Museum of Art, Los Angeles, CA

The Metropolitan Museum of Art, New York, NY

MOCA Grand Avenue, Los Angeles, CA

Musée d'Art Moderne et Contemporain, Geneva, Switzerland

The Museum of Modern Art, New York, NY

Nora Eccles Harrison Museum of Art, Logan, UT

Norton Simon Museum, Pasadena, CA

Phoenix Art Museum, Phoenix, AZ

San Francisco Museum of Modern Art, San Francisco, CA

Smithsonian American Art Museum, Washington, DC

Whitney Museum of American Art, New York, NY

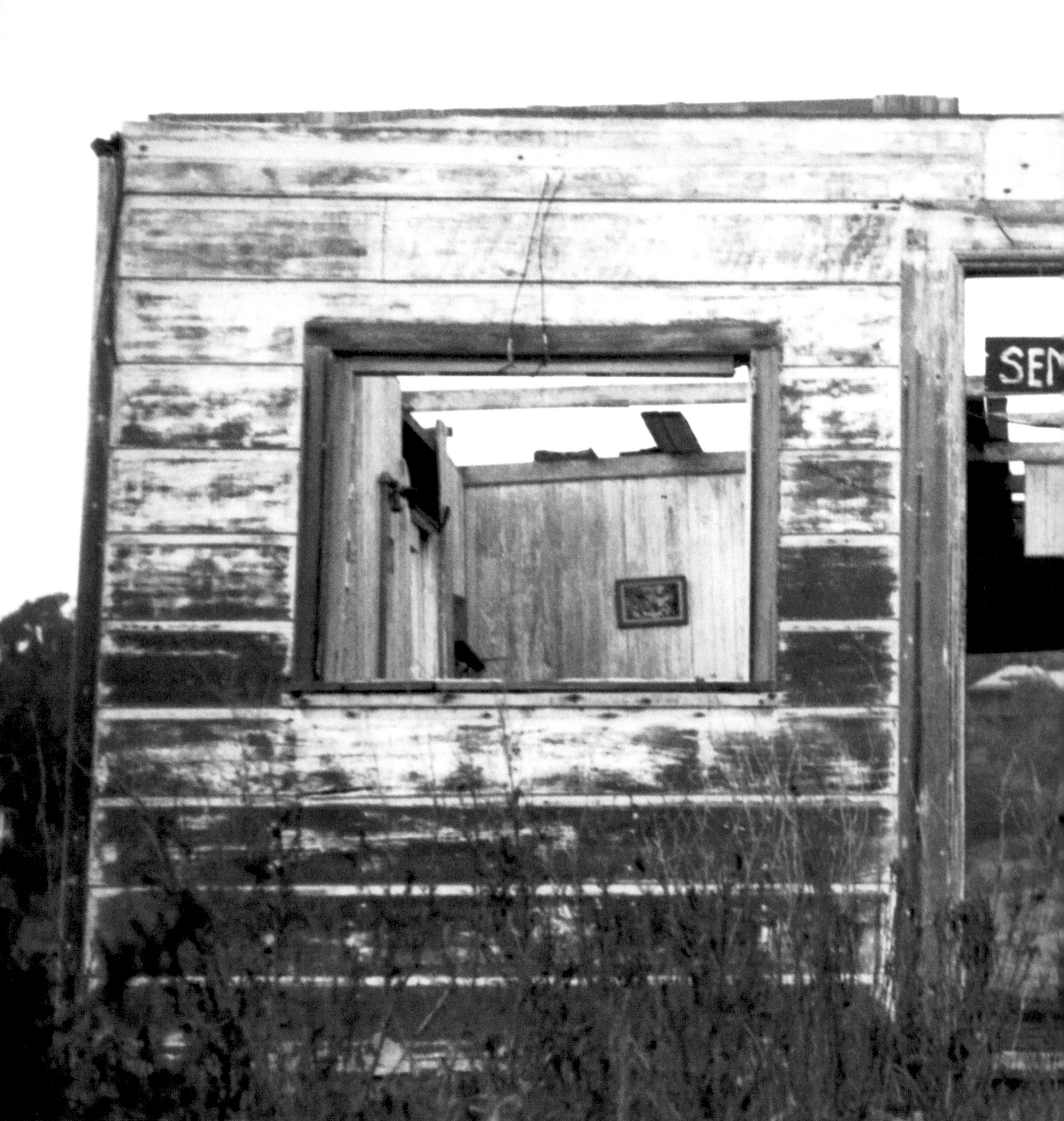

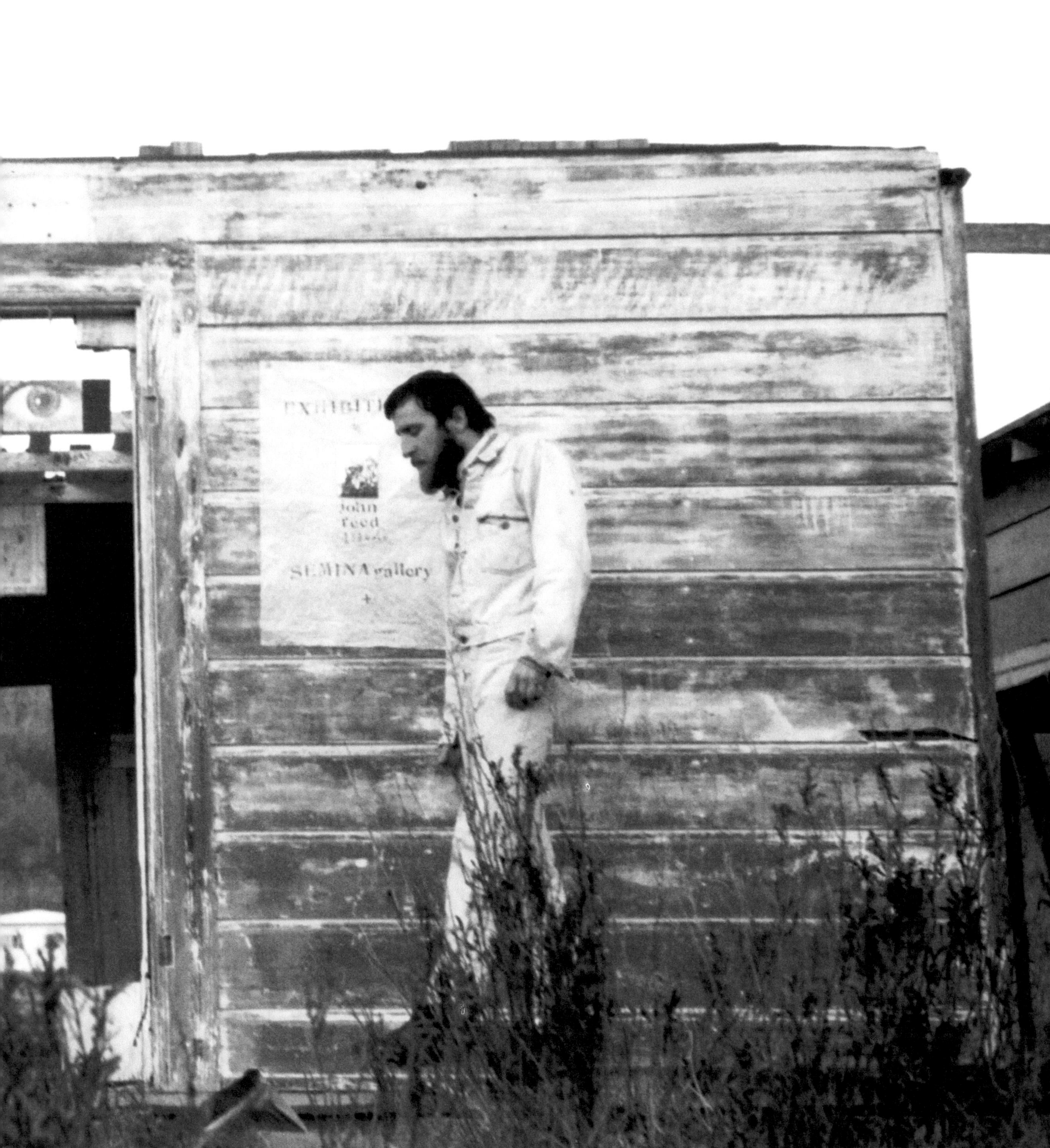
EXHIBIT
john
reed
SEMINA gallery

BIOGRAPHIES

Tosh Berman is a writer, a poet, and the publisher of TamTam Books. He has written three titles: *Tosh: Growing Up in Wallace Berman's World*, *Sparks-Tastic: Twenty-One Nights with Sparks in London*, and a book of poems, *The Plum in Mr. Blum's Pudding*. Berman served as executive director and curator at Beyond Baroque Literary Arts Center in Venice, California. He is the son of Wallace Berman and Shirley Berman.

Andrew Lampert is a New York City–based artist, writer, archivist, and primary in the firm Chen & Lampert. His work has been exhibited at the Whitney Museum of American Art, Centre Pompidou, Getty Museum, New York Film Festival, Toronto International Film Festival, and International Film Festival Rotterdam, among many other venues. The former curator of collections at Anthology Film Archives, he has edited numerous books on artists, including Tony Conrad, George Kuchar, Harry Smith, and William Wegman. Lampert is a monthly columnist for *Art in America*. His second album, a duet with the musician Chris Corsano, is forthcoming.

Saul Ostrow is an independent curator and critic. Since 1985 he has organized more than eighty exhibitions in the United States and abroad. His writings have appeared in art magazines, journals, catalogues, and books in the United States and Europe. In 2010, along with David Goodman and Edouard Prulhiere, he founded the not-for-profit Critical Practices Inc. as a platform for critical conversation and cultural practices. His forthcoming book *Formal Matters* will be published by Elective Affinity. He served as art editor at *Bomb* magazine, coeditor of Lusitania Press (1996–2004), and editor of the book series Critical Voices in Art, Theory and Culture (1996–2006), published by Routledge. He has an MFA in studio practices from the University of Massachusetts, and from 1968 to 1996 was a practicing artist.

Anne Waldman is a poet, performer, professor, curator, and cultural activist. In 1966 she helped found, and until 1978, run the Poetry Project at St. Mark's Church in New York City, and in 1974 she cofounded, with Allen Ginsberg and Diane di Prima, the Jack Kerouac School of Disembodied Poetics at Naropa University in Colorado. The author of more than fifty publications of poetry, including the recent *Trickster Feminism*, she is the recipient of the Poetry Society of America's Shelley Memorial Award and a Guggenheim Fellowship, and has served as a Chancellor of the Academy of American Poets. Recent publications include *Bard, Kinetic*, published by Coffee House Press, and the coedited anthology *New Weathers: Poetics from the Naropa Archive*, published by Nightboat Books.

Published on the occasion of the exhibition

Off the Grid at TOTAH, New York, September 8–November 6, 2021

Editor: TOTAH
Managing Editor: Sophia McKinnon
Copy Editor: Chris Peterson
Artwork photography: Julia Gillard, New York; Karl Puchlik, Kohn Gallery, Los Angeles

Excerpt from Hermann Hesse, *Steppenwolf*. Translated by Basil Creighton. New York: Picador, 2002.

First edition published in 2024

Edition of 1000

TOTAH
183 Stanton Street
New York NY 10002

Acknowledgments: Tosh Berman, Shirley Berman, Steve Hanson, Samuel Jablon, Nicole Knyfd, Michael Kohn, Michael Kohn Gallery, Sam Mellon, Lun*na Menoh, Nicola Tranquillino

"SCRY TOWARD AUGURY" by Anne Waldman coedited with Sophia McKinnon

Design by
Arielle Zoeller
Brooklyn, New York

Printed by
Grafice Veneziane
Venice, Italy

ISBN 978-1-7343045-6-5